QUIET
TOUGHNESS
Accelerate Your Success

Chuck Bushbeck

Quiet Toughness: Accelerate Your Success
by Chuck Bushbeck, as told to and arranged by EF Courtright

Year of the Book
135 Glen Avenue
Glen Rock, PA 17327

ISBN 13:   978-1-088661-18-5

Cover art: Brian Courtright

Cover photo: Jesse Biddle, Atlanta Braves pitcher. Used with permission.

The information in this book is meant to supplement, not replace, proper sports training. Like any activity involving physical and environmental factors, sports pose some inherent risk. The author and publisher advise readers to take full responsibility for their safety and know their limits. Do not take risks beyond your level of experience, aptitude, training, and comfort level.

To all the athletes and individuals I've had the privilege of coaching and training,
May you continue to inspire others throughout your life, just as you have inspired me.

TABLE OF CONTENTS

FOREWORD

I've been working with Chuck Bushbeck since I was fifteen – more than twelve years now. We met way back in 2006. My dad and I were looking for someone in the Philadelphia area who could maybe help get me to the next level of pitching. Chuck Bushbeck and his partner Chuck Bechtel are part of a handful of people who helped me become a major league pitcher. I don't think there's any question that if I hadn't started working with Chuck right then at that point in my development as an athlete I wouldn't have been a first-round pick in the 2010 amateur Major League Baseball draft.

In those early days when I was still a gangly doofus teenager, Chuck worked out of what we called his Rocky Balboa Hole-in-the-Wall, a cinder block storage building in Northeast Philadelphia. The lighting was a bit dim, I always felt kind of crammed into such a small space, and it was cold in the winter and hot in the summer.

Chuck broke me down and re-built me over the course of about two years - both physically and mentally. We would often end bullpen sessions with a long discussion about the physics of being a baseball player or the mind-body dilemma that all athletes have to face. Sometimes he'd give me a lecture on what it really means to be mentally prepared or how to have a balanced approach to success and working hard. I listened. Occasionally I didn't fully agree or I had trouble understanding. That didn't matter. Over the years I've learned that sometimes you're not ready to hear what you need to know until later on down the road.

No matter what, I'm so grateful for all the wisdom Chuck has imparted to me. He is an incredibly positive person who's demeanor and intensity are contagious. He didn't just make me a better athlete, he has helped me become a better person.

One of the things I admire most about Chuck is that he never wants to stop learning and pushing himself. Every off-season I would head over to Northeast Philly to work with him and his lessons would be clearer, more refined, and even more profound. I was always a work-in-progress for Chuck and his team. Truthfully, he has been a work-in-progress for himself as well.

So, after years of listening to him talk through his ideas about becoming a high-performing athlete devoted to excellence (and a high-performing human being devoted to the same), I'm very happy that he's put it all down here in *Quiet Toughness*. Much of what he taught me can be found in these pages. I can't guarantee you'll make it all the way to the major leagues, but I know that reading this book will help you find your way to new levels of confidence and higher mental and emotional frequencies that will help you in your quest to live a great life.

—JESSE T. BIDDLE
Atlanta Braves Relief Pitcher
Spring 2019

PREFACE

Have you ever thought of an old friend you haven't seen for a while, and then a few days later, run into them in the grocery store? Have you had moments where you're somewhere you've never been before, yet everything about your surroundings is familiar? Or what if you're an athlete on the playing field, and in an instant you somehow snatch an uncatchable ball out of mid-air?

From the beginning of time, these odd coincidences have plagued human kind, so much so, that we developed words and phrases to describe them. Things like *karma*, *destiny*, *fate*, *mind over matter*, *Murphy's Law*, *Catch-22*, *déjà vu*, *superstition*, or *Zen*. Whether the outcome is positive or negative, we can't deny these strange occurrences exist. We're surrounded by them every day.

But are they really just odd coincidences, or can they be explained by something greater?

Throughout history, civilizations have used things like religion and philosophy to rationalize the inexplicable. Think of the Greeks and Romans with their many Gods, meditating Tibetan monks, Japanese Reiki healers, Native American rain dances, or the astrologically advanced sundials built by the Mayans. Would any of these cultures have continued such beliefs and practices for centuries if no results were ever achieved?

Today many experts support theories about the intelligent design of our world and the life which inhabits it. Some attribute this to an omnipotent, compassionate God, and I am one of them. But whether you believe God exists is irrelevant to the purposes of this book. No one can deny the intricate makeup of the universe—everything from the unique binary DNA of each creature on earth to the vast solar system that surrounds us.

Regardless of your viewpoint, we all seek to define who we are and how we came to be. We utilize sciences such as quantum physics or quantum electrodynamics, the study of the behavior of matter at microscopic levels. We discuss topics such as epigenetics and cell biology. The ultimate goal of these scientific disciplines is to provide humankind with a better understanding of our physical and mental capabilities.

While I am not a scientist, I have studied the above-mentioned sciences extensively in order to apply them to my own life. Through research, I came to understand our existence from a much different perspective than what I'd previously believed. For me, these sciences are the "game changer," and the beginning of what you'll learn in this book. Note, however, that we merely touch upon them here. Should you be interested in pursuing your own research, I've included a number of links and resources in the Appendix.

My expertise comes from the B.A. I hold from Villanova University with a concentrated study in the areas of psychology, sociology, and philosophy, as well as 30+ years of working with clients.

I also have a profound love of sports. This is a result of being engaged in sports throughout my life, beginning at a tender age with little league, and on through college and early adulthood as a professional placekicker. In addition, for 11 years I was an Associate Scout for the Los Angeles Angels.

While observing many promising athletes, I saw a need. To help fulfill that need, I opened the Full Armor training facility in Northeast Philadelphia. From there I've been honored to individually train many young people striving to achieve their dreams. In working with these rising stars, I was able to utilize my experience and studies, not only in behavioral health but also in the sciences, to develop the program I call "RedOps."

The idea behind the name came from military Black Operations – more commonly known as BlackOps, the covert assignments of government intelligence. I like to think of RedOps as covert life intelligence. And "red" because all human beings bleed.

Every day athletes work hard, running, lifting weights, and honing their physical skills under the direction and motivation of coaches like myself. But I propose that there is more to becoming the best athlete one can be than just the physical. An often overlooked mental aspect also exists – a mental aspect that coincides and connects with universal energy.

RedOps is an overlapping five-tool process that enables us to channel energy and use it to rise above ordinary physical limitations. I know it works, because I've seen it work, not only in the athletes I train, but in my own life. The five chapters following this Preface, detail the "what," "why," and "how" of each tool.

While this program is geared toward athletes, it is in no way limited to sports. Quiet Toughness, the manifestation of utilizing RedOps, affects all facets of life – family, career, friendships, business acquaintances, as well as mental and physical health. This is about all of us finding a new way to look at our existence, enjoy our relationships, engage with our environment, and discover life's true bliss.

1 | ENERGY AND INFORMATION

Look closely into the eyes of a pure hitter at the plate facing a 97 mph fastball. The level of focus and confidence he exudes comes from being "in the zone." There are no doubts, no second thoughts or hesitation. For that hitter, the ball is no longer a beast to be slayed. It has become a slow-moving target that, through a transfer of energy, he bends to his will. His bat makes the connection, the crack resounds, and the ball soars.

Is it hogwash? No. Professional athletes will tell you this time and time again. For anyone who has been in a similar situation, the feeling is real – the split-second change in the physical realm, the shift of consciousness, and the slow motion-like transformation of the moving ball.

We don't have to be a major league ballplayer to tap into this elevated sense of realty. We can do it at any time. The question is how? The first step is to have a better understanding of the vibrational energy that drives our world.

WHAT

Quantum physics and cell biology tell us that everything – from the smallest atom on earth to the immense vastness of the universe – is made up of energy. Many organisms exist on our planet, and human beings are one of them. While other species are dependent upon instincts for survival, humans are far less discerning. For us, the goal is not only to survive, but to flourish. Our continual search for self-improvement differentiates us. In other words, we choose to use our intellect to effect change in our environment for the sole purpose of better accommodating our needs.

Every person has an energy stream. Different cultures use diverse terminology to describe it. Some call it an "aura," others use words like "spirit" or "soul." I like the terms "God-consciousness," "inner being," or "higher mind." Throughout this text I'll also refer to this energetic aspect of humanity as "vibration" or "frequency."

Regardless of the words used, we have a problem. We've encountered a roadblock, one that our intricate, absorbing, and intelligent minds have created, to our detriment.

Somewhere along the line, we concluded that there is a separation between our physical and spiritual beings. Nothing could be further from the truth. In reality our physical and spiritual sides are totally dependent upon each other. A deficit in either will affect the performance of both. For most of humankinds' existence, the connection between the two couldn't be supported by evidence. We're fortunate that today, modern science is proving otherwise.

Let's step back for a moment and think of universal energy. We know how powerful that energy is. Utilizing its force alone, we can take 15,000 pounds of mass and make it accelerate and stop. Although we can't see the energy, we know it's there. It's like a field of power surrounding us at all times.

This field doesn't judge our behavior, it only responds to it. That is because the universe is always in balance. Einstein's basic theory was that there is a perfect balance in nature between energy and matter. This can't be created or destroyed, only changed. Take away some energy and you get more matter. Take away matter, and energy replaces what's missing. The total is a constant.

Scientists have taken the nucleus – the brain of a cell – out of the cell, with the expectation that the cell would die. But it didn't. Instead it realized its new surroundings and adapted.

This same thing happens with certain earthly creatures. For example, if you cut off an earthworm's head, it will still gravitate toward food, and eventually regrow its brain. From a microscopic level, separated electrons functioned comparably, and when different interference patterns were added, the electrons reactions were altered. Further experiments revealed that even the observers' energy had an effect on the electrons movement, again causing amended results.

At Princeton University, the day before 9/11, scientists noticed an unusual spike in the earth's vibrational measurements. A consciousness had disrupted the meters, but no one present at Princeton knew what would happen the next day. Some people out in the world did, however. This tells us that our energy is continually being cast out into the field, and at the same time, the field is sending energy back to us.

Through epigenetics, we know that our perception of reality is what makes us who we are. From this, our disposition – or what we would call our temperament – is created. That temperament becomes our energetic frequency, which constantly attracts and repels the energy surrounding us.

Think of north and south pole magnets. If they're too far apart, you can still see they have an attraction, but the force is just not strong enough to pull them fully together. As the distance between them gets closer, the strength of the attraction increases, and when they collide, it becomes difficult to pull them apart. This is a mirror of how our connection with universal energy works.

Another way to look at it is like radio waves. We are continually broadcasting and receiving signals, with the tuner being our emotion or feelings.

Understanding these concepts is critical to allowing the principles of RedOps to enhance performance, encourage positive interaction, and allow our lives to shine with Quiet Toughness.

WHY

For centuries we have searched for ways to promote physical health and extend both the quality and quantity of life. While "Eastern" medicine continued down the path of natural healing and the exploration of the mind's control over the body, "Western" medicine elected to seek out external sources. With the discovery of miracle drugs like aspirin and penicillin, we continued to pursue artificial means to treat illness and lengthen lifespans. We have watched generation after generation doing research to find the perfect injection or pill that will solve our health issues.

If I told you there was a medication you could take that would allow you to perform at the highest level, have clarity of thought, peace of mind, and a healthy body, you would certainly consider it, wouldn't you?

Unfortunately the miracle medication doesn't exist. This doesn't mean, however, that it's not possible to have that kind of ultimate fulfillment. Remember, medication doesn't solve problems. It treats symptoms, but rarely addresses the underlying cause. The same holds true for everything we try to accomplish in our lives. We spend a great deal of time looking for quick fixes instead of learning, and then putting into practice, the mental discipline required for success. Sometimes quick fixes can disrupt the energy flow, and that is the last thing we want.

Our higher mind creates.

Our physical mind analyzes.

Our heart synthesizes.

Traditional thinking has told us that our brains are the highest functioning organ in our bodies. Today, scientists know this is, in fact, not the case. Cell biology proves that our brains and hearts are made up of the same properties. What's fascinating about these studies is that they show the heart is up to 100 times more powerful than the brain. That means the heart runs at a higher vibrational frequency.

So then it follows that while cognitive ability and thought process is important, feeling and emotion have an even greater impact on our spiritual selves and the reality of life as we perceive it.

Think of it this way: our brains don't lead us. They're the computer that dissects the data coming into our hearts.

Another way to break this down is: Our higher mind *creates*. Our physical mind *analyzes*. Our heart feels or *synthesizes*.

Have you ever watched a video of the metronome experiment? Thirty-two metronomes, arranged together in rows, and all set at the same speed (beats per minute), are "started" at different times. Because they're not started at the exact same moment, the little levers switch back and forth and are not synchronized. It sounds like multiple clocks ticking.

But then, over a matter of mere minutes, somehow the levers synchronize until they're all flopping back and forth in exactly the same direction at the same time. The ticking sounds like perfectly in-step marching soldiers.

Remember they were set at the same speed, so if each kept their speed, they "should" continue on and never synchronize, right?

Perhaps now you're thinking, the ticking was marginally off per metronome. This would mean, as more time passed, eventually they'd grow out of sync again. Nope. Once in sync, they remained in sync. This proves again how strong the energy is in our atmosphere. Like the metronomes, when our bodies and minds are in sync, disease is non-existent. And to be "in the zone," our hearts and minds must also be in harmony.

This is not just religion and philosophy anymore. Science now realizes the significance of our energetic sides, and how they are connected to universal energy.

HOW

In the formative years of our lives – from the moment the soul enters the mother's womb to age six – our only purpose is to gather data. We spend the days adjusting to our surroundings and exploring our environment. The information obtained is analyzed by our subconscious mind, and shapes our temperament.

The subconscious mind makes up 95% of who we are, how we react to various situations, and how we deal with stress and other obstacles thrown in our way. The lessons learned in those formative years stay with us forever and determine our reactions to outside stimulus. This doesn't mean we can't modify our reactions. It means that in order to do so, we need to recognize, and be cognizant of, the origins of our motivation.

A stumbling block we encounter in our culture is the emphasis placed on the acquisition of "things." We've lied to ourselves repeatedly by believing our "things" will bring happiness and fulfillment, when more often our "things" become distractions that knock us off the desired path.

If your reason for wanting to succeed as a professional athlete, or in any other endeavor, is to live in a mansion and drive a Lamborghini, you may find yourself feeling empty. Ask any successful person, and they will confirm their greatest joy hasn't come from their "things." It has come from performance, or being "in the zone."

> *We must think of ourselves as fully spiritual beings living out a life in human form.*

As an athlete, you've worked hard to get yourself physically prepared, but do you really want to go into battle wearing only half your armor?

Whether you're an aspiring athlete, or someone seeking positive life change, the RedOps approach is designed to help you get there. But like that miracle pill, it isn't free. It takes planning and effort. You will need to place the same emphasis on your mental preparedness as you have already placed on the physical, because as science proves, everything you receive in life is directly influenced by the energy you give off.

Another way to state this is by the old adage, "You reap what you sow." The fact that this phrase was originally written over 2,000 years ago is proof that our ancestors recognized these same concepts. They just didn't have the science to explain them.

The ultimate goal of RedOps is for us to allow negative energy to dissipate and to attract higher frequency energy. This puts us on an elevated plane where higher frequency energy flows back to us, allowing us to perform better, not just in sports, but in every nuance of our lives.

> *We're less than 1% particle, and more than 99% wave.*

The first step to attracting higher vibrational energy is changing the way we look at our makeup. Most of us think, as humans, we're merely physical beings with a brain that controls everything we do. We're like robots with a motherboard in our heads. And we believe maybe we have a spiritual element interwoven into our physical selves, but that spiritual piece is just a very small part.

What if we switch that up and take our physical mind out of the equation? What if I told you that in actuality, we're less than 1% particle, and more than 99% wave? If this is true, then we're exactly the opposite of what we've always believed. From here on out, I propose that rather than thinking of ourselves as human beings with an inkling of spirituality, we begin thinking of ourselves as fully spiritual or energetic beings living out a life in human form.

Using this premise, as a spiritual being connected to the energy field around us, there would be no limitation to what we can do. That is because our spiritual selves are in constant communication with the energy field. Our spiritual selves, or our higher minds, know us better than we know ourselves and are always looking out for our best interests.

The only question that remains is how does the human part of our mind improve the way it communicates with our spiritual self to attain results? Or, in other words, how do we truly tap into our Quiet Toughness?

In the next chapter – Mindfulness – we will delve more deeply into vibrational frequencies and how they impact us, both negatively and positively.

2 | MINDFULNESS

Imagine you're driving your car on your way to the gym. Suddenly the engine makes a guttural noise and stalls. You're able to roll enough to pull over at the curb. Once there, you try to start the car again, to no avail. Next, you pop the hood, but can't tell what the problem is. Your only option is to call AAA (fortunately you have AAA). They say they'll send a tow truck, but it will be an hour or more before it can get there.

What are you thinking and feeling at this point? And what are you going to do while you wait?

Choice #1: Sit in the car, cuss a few times, contemplate what a pain in the butt this is, moan about your ruined day, and moan some more about how much money you're going to have to shell out for repairs.

Choice #2: Look around at your surroundings and notice a restaurant across the street. The place looks interesting, and you've never been there before. Knowing you have at least an hour to kill, you lock up your car and head over. You sit at the bar, have a beer, chat with the fascinating people you've just met, and enjoy a great meal.

We all have the free will to make choices. The question is... what choices are you going to make, and how will those choices affect the energy field? What kind of energy do you want the field to send back to you?

17

Never underestimate the power of the mind, and remember the sway of positive thought is not a myth. With RedOps we continually send out positive energy so that in return, that's what the energy field reflects back to us.

WHAT

Part I: Mental Awareness

As an athlete, you spend an inordinate amount of time physically preparing for your sport. But being mentally prepared is just as important, if not more so.

> *When we send out positive energy, that's what the energy field reflects back.*

Think of the energy field, and what you project into it. If you want to turn your dreams into reality, then you must project positive energy, so that positive energy echoes back. Conversely, if you spend your time thinking about what you don't want, then that is what will echo back.

To illustrate, think of modern technology and the Cloud. The Cloud stores information so that we can access it from any of our devices. But the Cloud can only give back what we've put into it. We must think of the energy field like the Cloud. The energy we put into it, whether positive or negative, can be retrieved.

Natural human tendency is to take credit for the good stuff that occurs in our lives, and find blame for the not-so-good stuff. One of the primary lessons in RedOps is accountability. You are responsible for your successes, just as you are responsible for your failures. You can blame the coach, the umpires, or the field conditions all you want, but that is merely a deflection. If you continually try to blame someone or something for your performance, you will never improve. Admitting to your actions, whether good or bad, and saying, "I alone am responsible for what happens to me," throws that energy stream up into the Cloud. The Cloud will hold onto that accountability for you. When it comes back to you, it becomes the force that drives you to success.

Part II: Physical Awareness

The above sounds great, right? You can be anything you want to be so long as you send the right energy to the Cloud. Perhaps you're thinking to yourself, "I want to be a great NFL quarterback and lead my team to the Superbowl more times than Tom Brady."

But then you look in the mirror. You're fully grown and only 5'4" tall. You weigh 140 pounds, and as you've been teased your whole life, you're "small-boned."

Here's the list of the top ten quarterbacks of all time in the NFL:

1) Joe Montana – 6'2", 205 pounds.
2) Tom Brady – 6'4", 225 pounds.
3) Peyton Manning – 6'5", 230 pounds.
4) Dan Marino – 6'4", 228 pounds.
5) John Elway – 6'3", 215 pounds.
6) Brett Favre – 6'2", 222 pounds.
7) Johnny Unitas – 6'1", 196 pounds.
8) Steve Young – 6'2", 215 pounds.
9) Drew Brees – 6'0", 209 pounds.
10) Terry Bradshaw – 6'3", 218 pounds.

I think you see where I'm going with this. You want to be one of the best quarterbacks in the NFL, but the greats were all over six feet tall. In fact, the smallest quarterback in modern-day professional football history (1980–present) was Doug Flutie, who was 5'10" and 181 pounds when he played.

The point is, the likelihood of a guy who's only 5'4" becoming the next great quarterback is pretty much nil.

Being smaller of stature, however, doesn't preclude you from excelling in sports. Think of the many sports where weight class plays a part, such as wresting or boxing. Your size won't prevent you from furthering your education, pursuing wholesome relationships, or choosing an exciting and satisfying career either. Doctors and lawyers, for instance, come in all shapes and sizes.

> *You are responsible for your successes, just as you are responsible for your failures.*

Even Darwinism – survival of the fittest – doesn't say bigger is better. This has often been taken out of context. Darwin never said the guy with the biggest muscles will prevail. Survival of the fittest is having the best ability to adapt to the environment. The way that translates with RedOps is how we can best cooperate with the energy field.

Ultimately we need to be conscious of, and reasonable about, physical limitations when setting goals and seeking positive response from the Cloud.

WHY

Recently I worked with a talented ball player who runs like a deer, has a great arm, plays excellent defense, and although he's not a power hitter, is reliable at bat. These skills should be more than enough to get him where wants to go. But this gifted athlete has another characteristic that has nothing to do with his physical skills – his not-so-nice locker room demeanor. People don't like being around him. The negative energy he gives off is contagious and adversely affects his teammates. What ball club wants that? This player's temperament alone is killing his chances of making it.

Scouts see hundreds of players, and all of them have great physical skills. If you're one of them, how do you differentiate yourself from the competition? Believe me when I tell you scouts don't just pay attention to great on-field play. They watch just as closely how a player carries himself. How does he handle a mistake? Does he bounce back and snag the next fly ball? Or does he roll his eyes, cuss, and blame a teammate for causing an error? After a strike, does he slam the bat on the ground, or does he show determination for the next pitch? A player's attitude and conduct make all the difference.

Another way to look at it is if a hitter goes to the plate thinking about what he shouldn't be doing, there's a pretty good chance he will do exactly that. If he gets up saying to himself, "Don't swing at a bad pitch. Don't pop up. Don't strike out," what do you think will happen?

Fear and doubt project into the energy field, just as forcibly as confidence does. When you get up knowing you've given 100% to your physical and mental preparation, you have no

21

doubts or second thoughts. If you maintain a picture of success in your mind, that success will come to you.

As we said before, this does sound great in theory. But now you're thinking, how the heck am I going to change the vibration I give off, when I'm barely aware it exists? It's a great question. Tackling any of life's challenges takes practice and so does broadcasting positive energy.

HOW

Tackling any of life's challenges takes practice, and so does broadcasting positive energy.

Have you ever heard of someone who wrote out their goals on a wall or a whiteboard? They wrote them boldly, in a place they'd have to look at every day. Eventually those goals became reality. Successful people do this a lot. They do it because it works. But how?

Remember we talked about the non-existent magic pill? Here is where this comes into play. You are your own magic pill, and it's only through your attention and focus that the pill can do its job. It goes something like this:

You ask for something, and the universe hears you. Now your job is to "get out of the way" and let the universe manifest what you asked for. This doesn't mean that the manifestation will be instantaneous, or that your world will suddenly change for the better. There will be a timeframe for whatever it is you're seeking to materialize.

Keep in mind, there are rarely quick fixes, and impatience can be a negative vibration that will lower the higher frequency. The higher the frequency – meaning the more positive the thought (so that we feel the experience as if it has already happened) – the easier it will be for what you ask to come to fruition.

The higher the frequency, the easier what you ask for will come to fruition.

If, by chance, you're a *Star Trek* fan, think of the Vulcans and how they communicate via mind meld. They understood this concept perfectly. Except they were missing one aspect that is critical – Vulcans suppress emotions.

All kidding aside, it is important to understand how our emotions affect our communication with the Cloud. This coincides with what we discussed about the heart in Chapter 1.

Generally speaking, it has been said that the difference between men and women is that men see things in black and white, and women run on emotion. Regardless of your gender, and the makeup of your character, we all feel emotion (except perhaps for psychopaths who are completely disconnected from their power, but that is a topic for another day).

Our feelings and emotions are the compass we use to navigate the waters of life.

Even the most level-headed realists, who may not show their feelings outwardly, are internally guided by emotion. Our emotions are what carry our energy. When we communicate with the Cloud, we're not just uploading our desires. We're uploading the feelings behind them. That emotion, whether positive or negative, is what the Cloud holds onto and downloads back to us.

In order to have a better of understanding of how feelings carry our energy, we have a scale similar to the Global Assessment of Functioning (GAF), utilized by psychiatrists and psychologists, but our "Emotional Scale" has been simplified to measure energetic frequency. This scale ranks emotions from the most desirable frequency (#1) to the least desirable (#22). Here is the list:

1) Joy/Appreciation/Empowerment/Freedom/Love
2) Passion
3) Enthusiasm/Eagerness/Happiness
4) Positive Expectation/Belief
5) Optimism
6) Hopefulness
7) Contentment
8) Boredom
9) Pessimism
10) Frustration/Irritation/Impatience
11) Being Overwhelmed
12) Disappointment
13) Doubt
14) Worry
15) Blame
16) Discouragement
17) Anger
18) Revenge
19) Hatred/Rage

20) Jealousy
21) Insecurity/Guilt/Unworthiness
22) Fear/Grief/Depression/Despair/Powerlessness

Ideally we'd like to stay at the highest frequency possible (#1) all the time, which isn't easy to do. One of the greatest impediments to maintaining high frequencies is having those high frequencies trampled upon by lower frequencies, like fear and doubt.

Figuring out your actual frequency is similar to finding the median in a list of numbers. For example, we experience #1, but also have plenty of #10 (frustration, impatience) going on at the same time. Our frequency will actually be #4 (positive expectation/belief) or #5 (optimism) on the scale. In other words, the lower frequency has a negative impact on the higher, causing our overall frequency to decrease.

The lower frequencies are what we call "resistance." They're like a clog in a pipe of running water.

Another difficulty to maintaining higher frequencies comes from habits. Habits are hard to break. Most of us have been programmed from the time we were young – those formative years we talked about – to be afraid and have doubts. Fear and doubt are like bad habits (clogged pipes). By allowing them to influence our actions for so long, ignoring or screening them out becomes tough.

Lower frequencies are like a clog in a pipe of running water.

The way to approach this is similar to how you'd work out to physically prepare for an event, except that this time you're dealing with mental preparation. You have to begin by policing yourself to allow your frequency to rise.

The change we are talking about has to come from your core. If you think about all your physical preparation, you know that the key is in developing your core muscles. Mental preparation is no different. The key to strengthening your mental approach to life is to strengthen your core belief system. If you send messages to the Cloud merely "hoping" you'll succeed, the doubts will be reflected back. However, if the messages you send to the Cloud are confident, then the energy you get back will be confident.

> *The energy field considers each of us to be a most beloved soul and will never do anything to harm us.*

The best way to raise confidence is by reminding ourselves, and therefore knowing, that the energy field is always compassionate. It considers each of us to be a most beloved soul and will never do anything to harm us. At all times, the only thing the field strives for is what's best for us.

Also keep in mind, the Cloud doesn't judge what we feel, but merely responds to it. Everything in our universe is energy and information. Everything in your life is the sum total of what you have put there. If you don't like what's there, the key is finding a solution. Then the change you seek will occur. Until we master this, we have to grit our teeth and deal with what's been created so far. To be successful in achieving your goals, you have to match your frequency with what you want. Think of it like a radio station, where you have to adjust the tuner to find the music you prefer.

How do we get our physical mind out of the way and let the higher mind attract? In the next chapter, we'll delve more deeply into one method that works well to help us tap into higher frequencies, and in turn manifest what we truly desire.

3 | INSPIRED ACTION

A few years ago, I was on my way to see a client who lived on an upper floor of an older apartment building. The only way to get there was by ascending several flights of steps. At the time, I wasn't physically unfit. I wasn't overweight. But I became so short of breath, I couldn't make it up those stairs.

This was the beginning of a battle with what doctors diagnosed as Cardiomyopathy, Heart Disease, and Congestive Heart Failure. They said the issues were a calcium build-up resulting from radiation treatments I'd had for lymphatic cancer 30 years before. Regardless, I was only 54 years old, and my heart was shot.

The first attempts to keep me alive were to unclog my arteries with stents. The arteries clogged again, and I had to be "re-stented." When they clogged a third time, it became apparent that my heart was worn out and wasn't going to last much longer. A heart transplant was my only hope. But even that didn't seem feasible. Surgeons didn't want to operate, because of complications from attaching my radiation damaged arteries. Without a new heart, doctors told me I'd survive at best, about nine months.

Not long after this devastating news, I happened upon a YouTube video of Dr. Joe Dispenza lecturing about the science of the mind. Considering my state of health, trying the meditation he recommended certainly couldn't hurt. So I did it. Every day.

I'll never forget a subsequent appointment I had with a Cardiac Specialist in Washington, D.C. I was scheduled for brachytherapy to radiate inside the clogged stents. Upon examining my arteries, the doctor was stunned. Only one of my stents seemed to have an obstruction. The other was clear.

I knew the mindfulness training was working. The doctor treated the clogged stent and left the clear one alone. Five months later, even though the cleared stent remained clear, the other began to clog again. I told my cardiologist the clog would be gone in six months.

Inspired actions begin with the proactive measures we take to raise our frequencies.

During the mindfulness training that followed, a thought was downloaded to me that led me to watch a video about natural supplements. The woman in the video had a recipe I copied. Within two days I felt a difference. I was breathing easier and had more energy, and I knew that meant my heart was getting itself back into shape.

When I returned to the hospital six months later, tests revealed that my heart was functioning normally. I told my doctor about the mental training I was doing, as well as the recipe I'd been taking. She said my efforts were most likely affecting the proteins my body produced. Combined with the neural transmitters, I'd created a coherence between my brain and my heart.

Inspired actions begin with the proactive measures we take to raise our frequencies. This can be done in different ways, but the result is the same – a change in the way we view the world, enabling our Quiet Toughness to prevail. For me, figuring out what inspired actions I needed to take started with meditation, which is why this chapter is dedicated to this topic.

WHAT

There are many types of meditation. Different instructors, organizations, and/or religions refer to them by different names. Appendix B at the end of this book contains several resources for a more in-depth look at the different methods. For our purposes we're going to narrow it down to two basic types: (1) Directed; and (2) Non-Directed.

Non-Directed Meditation is used primarily for clearing the mind of all outside interference and connecting with the energy field. It is most helpful for relieving stress and becoming more in tune with higher level emotive states, such as compassion, contentment, joy, and appreciation.

Directed Meditation will also help attain higher level emotive states, but this is where the focus is on the future and the successes we seek. In effect, it's about connecting with the energy field in order to direct our destiny. These successes could be within relationships, careers, sports, health issues, or any other goal we've set for ourselves.

Both methods have a positive impact on our ability to control our frequency and our interaction with the field.

WHY

Meditating is a process that puts us more closely in touch with our inner beings, our spiritual selves, or our subconscious, higher minds. The terminology you prefer is up to you. What matters is the goal – to connect with the energy field so that positive energy will flow back.

From the time we're young – our formative years – we learn competition. In some people, competitiveness is so strong it drives almost everything they do. In others, competitiveness is less intense, but it still exists to a degree. Meditation removes competition and replaces it with cooperation. Cooperation allows us to connect, and cooperate, with the energy field. It also enables us to move up on the emotional scale.

> *Meditating is a process that puts us more closely in touch with our higher minds.*

Science tells us if we close our senses to the physical world, stress hormones (*cortisol* and *epinephrine*) reduce, the heart flows freely, and we become more tranquil. In addition, neurological activity increases, changing the psychological structure of the brain, and alkalinity is produced in the body.

Studies have shown that alkaline enzyme production can improve the immune system and even have the power to destroy cancer cells. The benefits of meditation have also been proven through experiments done on individuals known to be spiritual masters. Meditation unleashed such super-human defense mechanisms that when these masters were purposely injected with the Ebola virus, it had no effect.

Whether you're dealing with health issues or merely seeking to improve your life, the meditative state enables you to reside more easily in a space of gratitude. Compassion, appreciation, joy, and love – the emotions we seek – become the center. They project into the energy field, and reflect back. This is where low self-esteem, doubt, fear, and feelings of unworthiness disappear. The result is not only peace, but confidence.

For people who have never meditated before, initially it will feel like work. That's okay. Start slowly. The first time, just try two or three minutes. The next day, try five minutes. You will find that the more you do it, the more you will want to do it. Think of yourself as a cell phone that needs to be plugged in every night to charge. That's what meditation will do for you – charge you, so that you're ready to face the next day (or the rest of the day, depending upon when you prefer to "charge").

HOW

For purposes of these instructions, we'll assume you haven't had any experience with meditation. If you have, then some of this may be repetitive, or my methods may differ from yours. There are many ways to reach a meditative state, and everyone must find what works best for them. If you have a system you're already comfortable with, there's no reason to change. How you get there is not as important as getting there. Below is a simple **4-step** process.

Step 1: Atmosphere and Position

The key to getting into a meditative state is relaxation. My preference is a dark, quiet room, with no distractions. Many people like to have white noise in the background – like the hum of a fan. Music, preferably without lyrics, can be used. But even something like the steady soft tick of a clock can work well. So does silence.

As for how to position yourself, Eastern schools of thought generally teach a lotus position (sitting cross-legged). Comfortable chairs can be as effective, and lying prone also works well. No matter what posture you take, it should require minimal muscle intervention to maintain. Being in an uncomfortable stance can be just as distracting as someone shouting in the next room.

Step 2: Breathing

Begin with two cleansing breaths. A cleansing breath is a deep, full inhale followed by a slow exhale. For the first one, take air in through the nose, executing as slowly as possible without making yourself uncomfortable. This inhale should fill your lungs and cause your chest to rise. Hold onto that breath for a few seconds. Don't force it, but don't exhale until it feels natural to do so. Then slowly let the air go through your mouth, allowing small amounts to escape at a time. Keep going until all the air is forced from your lungs. Repeat for the second breath. This helps to relax you and slow your heart rate.

Step 3: Muscles

The goal is to relax the muscles, so that all focus can center in the mind. There are many different methods to achieve muscle relaxation. I'll describe three – **Beam of Light**, **Silver Cord**, and **Third Eye** – below. These can be used individually or in tandem. It doesn't matter which method you use, or even if you do something entirely different than what's suggested here. The point is to do whatever it takes to get your muscles in a fully relaxed state.

Beam of Light

Imagine a bright beam of light entering your body through your feet. We begin with the toes and move up the body to the head. The light travels slowly as it goes from muscle to muscle, touching each one in turn. As the light hits each muscle, tense that muscle briefly, and then release. Applying this tension allows you to acutely focus on that particular muscle. Continue through your body, not skipping any muscles, until the light has fully passed through and exited your head.

Silver Cord

It's been said that when someone dies, a silver cord can be seen coming from the top of their head. This is the soul, departing from the body and being taken up into the energetic plane. In death, the cord severs from the head. Of course, you're not dying when you meditate, but you can still let the cord stretch from the top of your head and connect with universal energy. As you feel this happening, you'll experience a pull from your body. It's the energy rising up from your solar plexus and permeating the rest of your muscles, up through your backbone, your neck, and out through the top of your head.

Third Eye

Another good way to help yourself drop into the no-space, no-time continuum, is to focus on your forehead between your two eyebrows. In Eastern religion this spot is called "the third eye." Concentrate on nothing but your third eye. As you do this, you're seeing into the energy field. The energy will push through your body, up from the solar plexus, through your backbone, your neck, and through your head. Then you let it go.

Don't forget to breathe. No matter which method used, while going through muscle relaxation, don't forget to breathe – deep full breaths, in through the nose and out through the mouth. You should be focused on your breathing at all times.

The result: No matter which method (or combination of methods) used, you will find yourself in a different state of awareness, a trance of sorts, as if you've stepped out of your own existence. You may experience a kind of lightheadedness, or feeling of floating. For some it feels like you're actually moving backwards. This is because you've released your physical reality and become one with your higher mind.

Step 4: Empty the Mind

Because you've been concentrating on breathing and muscle relaxation, at this point, your mind should already be empty. You should be thinking of nothing, except breathing and either the beam of light, silver cord, or your third eye.

Now, imagine your mind is like a black hole, void of any trouble or worry. If you find yourself drifting to daily grind stuff – the stuff you think about regularly during the course of a day, i.e., a project due at work, or behavioral troubles your child is having in school – let those thoughts dissipate. Sometimes you may have to channel yourself back, and that's okay. Concentrate on breathing and the beam of light, silver cord, or third eye.

At times the light may have to pass through your body a second time, the silver cord may have to stretch out again, or your third eye may have to re-open. The goal is to empty your mind so that the only thing available to fill it is emotional vibration. You're tapping into the energy that surrounds you – the energy in the room, and the energy of the universe.

From this point, we can go one of two ways, depending upon whether you're doing Directed or Non-Directed Meditation.

For Non-Directed Meditation, drift to a place of appreciation. What are the things in life you're thankful for? Keep it simple, like that you have a roof over your head and food to eat, even if the roof leaks, or the only food you can afford is Ramen Noodles. You're not starving, right? So be grateful.

You'll begin to sense higher level feelings being downloaded to you.

If you have other things to be thankful for, like a committed spouse and precious children, be thankful for them, not allowing anything negative to intervene. So what if your wife nags you to take out the trash, or your children talk back sometimes?

Again, keep it simple. Despite the difficulties, deep down you truly are thankful these people are in your life. You love them. Let the energy field feel how much.

The stressful things in your life will surface, and that's okay. But now, instead of feeling despair (#22 on the emotional scale) about something that happened, allow yourself to rise up a few notches to merely disappointment (#16).

What if a project in your job bores (#8) you? Can you raise that emotion up to hopefulness (#6)? Perhaps you can concentrate on the outcome of the project and what the finished product will produce. Doing this might even get you up to expectation (#4).

Over time, as you push these emotions up the scale, you will find that life's difficulties lessen in severity. You'll find yourself seeking alignment and cooperation. You'll also discover an ability to cope even under the most trying of circumstances.

Let your energy out into the field, so that the field can send it back at a higher level. Over time, you'll begin to feel the higher level feelings being "downloaded" to you.

For Directed Meditation, begin the same way, but now you're concentrating on something specific, something you want to accomplish. Let your emotions surround whatever it is. Imagine the success and completion as if whatever it is has already happened. In the field it has already happened. The feeling of "being in the zone" goes along with this.

For example, let's say you're writing a book, something you've dreamed of doing for years. What do you want to happen with that book? You want to get it published, and you want it to sell, right? Imagine yourself talking with the literary agent who will represent you. Imagine yourself at a book signing, with people coming up to the table to talk to you. You project the emotions associated with these desires out into the energy field, and the energy field hears them.

Will things turn out exactly as you imagine? Not always. In our example, fast forward two years. The bookstore looks entirely different than the one in your head, and maybe not as many people are there as you'd believed would be. So what? You're signing the books you wrote, right? The point is you sent out what you wanted to happen into the field, and you remained faithful and confident that someday your desires would materialize. And they did. The most important thing here is the emotion. You're excited at your book signing, so that's the emotion you've sent out and what creates the manifestation.

Perhaps you're thinking, "I'm gonna meditate about winning the lottery." This thought is coming from your physical mind, not your higher mind. If you don't win, this will only lead to personal frustration.

Thoughts lead to emotion.

Emotion. leads to feeling.

Feeling is the vibration.

In cases like this, what you'll find instead of realizing what you ask for, is that doors will close. You won't be able to push them open, because you've created an energetic disturbance in the field.

More focused energy work needs to be applied. This is about emotional-feeling connection. You emotionally connect with universal energy, and the universe answers the moment you ask. It will download all the information and direction you'll need, so that physically, you will know what to do to make your dreams become reality.

Just remember, it's all about the giving and receiving of feelings. Thought leads to emotion, emotion leads to feeling, and feeling is the vibration.

How long should you meditate? As long as you want. Some people meditate several hours a day, and others only for a few minutes. What matters more is what we choose to put our time toward, then making the commitment and following through. There is no question in my mind that you will benefit from the results.

As you come out of your meditation, you will find thoughts being downloaded to you. They're not thoughts from your physical mind. These are ideas and plans being revealed to you. These revelations will tell you the book to read, the person to see, the teacher to go to, the song to listen to, the show to watch. These downloads will provide everything you need to inspire you to move toward achieving your goals.

At the beginning of this chapter I told the story of my failing heart. I meditated every day for months, focusing on my arteries. In my mind I saw them clear, the blood freely flowing. I also concentrated on my family, seeing my children's futures filled with happiness and contentment. I did the same for my athletic clients.

When it was time for my appointment, after I told the doctor my heart would be better, I knew before I arrived that I'd done what I'd set out to do. My heart was healthy again, and it's still going strong.

What inspired actions do you need to take to improve your performance on and off the field, and tap into your Quiet Toughness? Meditate and find out.

4 | CONTRAST

I would like to tell you two stories about friends of mine, Stephen and Jack.

Stephen

Stephen is a well-educated financial analyst. He graduated college and sought out his first job. It was a good one, with a nice starting salary. He worked there for six months, until one day he was called into his boss's office. The boss fired him. But it wasn't so bad. Before long, Stephen found another position with another company.

He got fired from that one too, as well as the third, fourth, and fifth positions he held. All told, over a course of seven years, Stephen was fired nine times. At the last six jobs, when he got the call to go to his boss's office, Stephen knew what would happen before he even opened the door.

He didn't know why he had such bad luck, but with each firing he fell deeper and deeper into depression. He didn't think he'd ever be successful in his chosen career.

A friend of his commiserated, and then dared Stephen to read a specific chapter from a self-help book every day for a year.

Stephen took his friend up on the dare and read that same chapter every day. Within the year Stephen had another new job. Fast forward several years. Not only did he excel in this position, but he moved up in the company, and now has a whole team of financial analysts reporting to him. In fact, everything Stephen wanted in life, both professionally and personally, came to fruition.

Jack

Jack is a businessman and a multimillionaire. Not too long ago he had a falling out with a business partner and is now embroiled in a bitter court battle. Jack says he's getting screwed, and he hates his life. Every day he worries about money. Every day he worries about whether his other partners and associates are also going to do something to screw him.

Jack says, "Even if I win in court, when this whole thing is over, I'll probably get sick and die, and never see a dime of the money my partner stole from me."

I have never seen anyone as stressed as Jack has been while going through this mess.

What are the morals of these stories? Stephen found something that cut through his inner turmoil, reached into his subconscious mind, and inspired him. And Jack... let's just hope and pray that someday Jack finds something to inspire him, too.

Our bodies are equipped to handle stress to a degree. Stress hormones like *cortisol* and *epinephrine* automatically release when needed.

Just like every other living being on the earth, we also have a built-in fight or flight mechanism. Think of a herd of gazelles in a meadow, contently eating grass. Suddenly a mountain lion darts toward them. The gazelles run, but one of them is slower and weaker than the rest, and not quick enough to outrun the mountain lion. The mountain lion gets the gazelle, and satisfied with his catch, doesn't chase the rest of the herd. As soon as the remaining gazelles realize the danger is over, they go back to grazing as if nothing untoward occurred.

Humans aren't wired this way. If a bunch of us were attacked and one of us killed, the rest would suffer, unable to let the distress of the moment go. Holding onto that kind of fear and guilt has its own way of tearing us apart.

The Western culture we adhere to doesn't teach the tools to help relieve stress.

It's like we're carpenters
trying to build a house
with a plunger and a toothbrush.

WHAT

Before we delve more deeply into contrast, I want to briefly recap.

- The world is made up of energy.
- We're spiritual beings, also made up of energy.
- We're here on this earth to create the life we want.
- In order to create the life we want, we must communicate with the energy field.

- The most effective way to communicate with the energy field is through meditation.
- The energy field projects back to us, everything we put into it, whether negative or positive.
- The energy field will download to us the information and direction we need in order for positive change to occur.
- The doors to our goals and dreams will open as our frequencies rise.

That all sounds good, but imagine for a moment if everybody followed these tools. Certainly everyone can't have everything they want, right? If everybody who wanted to be a professional athlete became one, then we'd have a lot of athletes on the field, and no fans in the stands.

Let's step back and look at this from a different perspective. Take two opposing teams getting ready for a championship game. For purposes of our example, let's say every player on those teams understands RedOps. Every player has projected positive energy into the field. Every player has envisioned a win, and because of this, every player is confident their team will prevail. Yet both teams can't win; one has to lose.

This is contrast, or perceived adversity. It occurs when what we're confident about doesn't manifest the way we want it to. Contrast can show up in many forms.

It can be a dip on the emotional scale. An example would be something you're optimistically anticipating. Maybe you're giving a speech, or singing a solo during a choral concert. You've worked hard, you're prepared and confident, but just before you go on stage, fear and doubt kick in. You lose your place in the middle of the presentation, or a frog gets in your throat mid-song and you croak out a bad note.

Another example of contrast is an obstacle thrown in your path. Imagine you have a tryout with a major league ball club. You've worked hard, you're prepared and confident. But then, the day before the tryout, while at practice, you break your thumb.

Contrast also asserts itself with timing. A project you've worked diligently on is completed. All you need is an investor to buy in. The investors you've approached, even though they've expressed interest, either don't call you back, or decide to turn you down. The date you expected your project to go live has come and gone, and you're still looking for investors.

So, why does contrast or adversity present itself? And when it does, what can we do about it? Read on.

WHY

Adversity exists to help us grow. It certainly helped Stephen grow. And Jack's story isn't finished yet. I'd like to illustrate this in another way, by sharing examples from my own life.

The first story I'd like to share occurred when I was twenty-one years old, before I had my degree, or gained life experience working in behavioral health. This was long before I'd ever heard of quantum physics or any of the other sciences mentioned in these pages. In fact, everything discussed in this book was unknown to me. I was pre-season all-American, going into my senior year of college at a Division I school as a starting placekicker. Football was everything to me, and all I wanted was to someday play

Adversity helps us grow.

professionally. I had the leg, the temperament, and was only one season shy of realizing my dream.

Two weeks before our opening game, I was diagnosed with Hodgkin's Lymphoma. My doctors told me I had to quit and go home. They said I needed surgery and radiation treatments, but there was no guarantee that the treatments would work. If they didn't, I was going to die.

I looked at it like, if I don't play this year, I might never get to play again. Lucky for me, I was surrounded by supportive coaches, teammates, and friends. I was sick as a dog, puking my guts up almost every day. I couldn't eat, and through the season lost more than 40 pounds. Sometimes, on really bad days, my teammates had to help me on and off the field, but I never missed a game. That season, somehow I kicked every extra point successfully, and even set a field goal record for my team.

What did I learn from this experience? It was one of the worst times of my life, but it was also one of the best. If it weren't for the cancer, I wouldn't have met or grown close to many incredible people who have had an indelible impact on me, and I wouldn't have realized my own strength – strength that carried me through later battles. This jarring obstacle put in my path, made me appreciate and value life as nothing else could.

There is a reason for every adversity we face, whether minor or significant. Why did my neighbor's dog crap on my lawn? Why did the traffic light have to change when I'm already late? Why did my heretofore sweet child talk back to his teacher and get himself suspended?

Even the seemingly inconsequential happenings can cause stress. But the universe is on our side. The reason we encounter things like this is to get us to come up to a higher frequency. Our inner guide is always pulling for us.

The radiation treatments I endured in 1981 left me with several other health issues, the heart problems I shared earlier being one of them. But this segues into the next story – something that happened about 10 years ago.

I was burnt out on social work, partly from dealing with too many heart-wrenching stories of abuse and neglect, but mostly because of the endless paperwork and red tape. I wasn't helping people anymore. All I was doing was pushing paper. I had started the Full Armor training facility, but because of my job, couldn't spend the time I wanted working with athletes. I was frustrated and torn between needing that steady paycheck and doing what inspired me.

Recognize contrast for what it is, and realize it has a purpose for the greater good.

Then, one weekend, I was pitching in a baseball game and got a terrible backache. I ended up going to the doctor, who discovered I had a tumor in my stomach. It should have been an easy surgery to remove, but something went wrong, and my stomach exploded. I went into septic shock and spent the next 28 days in the ICU, most of the time incoherent and hallucinating. I almost died again. The few moments of lucidity I had, I remember thinking, "I'm not ready to go yet."

I believe this was a wake-up call, so to speak. It was the only way the universe could get my attention and make me realize how negative I'd become because of my job. I got better,

> *By using the techniques of RedOps, you can prune existing neurological pathways to create a newer, healthier life.*

finally, and let the downloads begin – downloads that told me I needed to change the path I was on. I needed to concentrate on the athletes, because that was where I could do the most good. I have never appreciated a message more, and I have never looked back.

Another way to think of contrast or adversity is that it is like friction, and it exists in every part of the world. The key is to recognize it for what it is, and realize it has a purpose, generally for the greater good.

A word of caution: Contrast could easily be confused with free will. For example, look at those who suffer from addiction. Contrast may put the obstacle – opioids, or a newly built casino – in our path, but contrast doesn't make us choose to take the drugs or gamble away our life's savings. Don't confuse contrast with free will. We all have the free will to make choices.

We make choices every day. The question we should ask ourselves is whether the choices we make are being decided by our physical mind or our higher mind?

When dealing with issues like addiction, the physical mind is running on autopilot, and has become dominant. Now your biology is controlling your choices, and will remain a constant, which is why addiction is so difficult to overcome. This is not necessarily your fault, but it is your responsibility to make changes.

Science shows us that we have the mechanisms to amend our biology. By using the techniques of RedOps, you can prune existing neurological pathways to create a newer, healthier life.

When we make choices with our higher mind, then the choices will never be wrong. The higher mind always works for our greater good.

Remember in Chapter 1 where we talked about Einstein's theory of energy and matter being a constant? Ask yourself this question: does matter control my mind? Or does my mind control matter? Without changing our energy, it will be nearly impossible to change unwanted circumstances. Quiet Toughness enables us to pull out of the world so that we can create the world we prefer.

How do we connect more succinctly with our higher mind, so that we can create different momentum and direction for our lives? How do we turn adversity into a lesson that will help us grow?

HOW

Do you recall the example of the broken down car in Chapter 1? You're on the side of the road, waiting for the AAA tow truck. You have two choices: (1) Whine and moan about how much your life sucks right then; or (2) Go across the street, get a bite to eat, meet some new people, and make the best of an unfortunate situation.

So how do we deal with contrast? We have the free will to make those decisions. The question is whether we want to stay in a positive emotional plane, and allow those amplifications to return to us. Or do we fall deeper to the negative?

I propose, if you choose not to dwell on the problem, but instead make the best of it, the issue with the car won't turn out to be that bad. Whereas, if you bemoan every second, have a sharp tongue with the AAA guy, and are still disgruntled at the repair shop, your car will most likely have more than one thing wrong with it, and the bill will be steep.

Did you know most heart attacks occur on Monday mornings? The theory is that these heart attacks are the result of stress – people going off to start another work week in a job they hate. According to studies, 99% of our problems are a direct result of stress, including maladies like migraines, cancer, and heart disease.

Traditional school of thought has always been recommendations of exercise and rest to lower stress levels. But people in chaos will more often only listen to what is pushing them the most – the obstacles causing the stress. They stay focused on the problem and never get out from under it. Think of poor Jack.

Recently I read about a guy who, even though he was never violent, always had a bad attitude. Every week this guy got in a fender bender. His frequency was made up of despair, confusion, and anger. These emotions were projected into the field, and sent back, leaving him stuck in a rut, experiencing those difficult and stressful frequencies day after day.

Have you ever known a person like that? I have. They hate their job, have nothing nice to say about their spouse and kids, their home is a mess, and so is their health. You regularly hear them say things like, "It's just my bad luck," and "My life sucks."

You might try to cheer them up with words like, "Look on the bright side..." No matter what bright side you may find amidst their troubles, their response is, "That won't work for me," or "Yeah, right."

Have you ever noticed that after being around this person for a while, when you part company, you're in a bad mood? Negativity is toxic. While you're with a negative person, their energy connects with yours, and brings your frequency down.

We encounter negative people every day. It's even worse when members of our families, or people we live with, are this way. Avoiding them is impossible.

Remember, if we're not conscious of what we're doing in the present moment, then we're falling into the learned behavior from our formative years. This is our subconscious behavior responding to current life situations.

Now, if 95% of our thought processes are subconscious, and our subconscious is unhealthy, then those thought processes are like an undetected computer virus, and we haven't installed the anti-virus protection yet. We're letting ourselves be brought down, and don't even realize it.

This is where we can raise our awareness. Recognize the negativity in others. Recognize our own, as well as why we might be drawn to negativity. Ask the question, "Why did I choose to be around this person to begin with?"

Then let Quiet Toughness meditation be the anti-virus software. Use the energy and information we now know, so that only higher frequencies resonate. By doing so, we promote cooperation with universal energy, and this leads us right into our last tool – *allowing*.

5 | ALLOWING

I knew a kid once who wanted to be a championship tennis player. He worked hard and improved his game. But there was a problem. His reason for this goal was merely to show off to his friends.

This is an example of self-motivation. It is not inspired action. His thought process was all physical, and not in cooperation with his higher mind or the energy field.

Do you know what happened? One day he decided being a great tennis player was too much work. He put down his racquet, and hasn't picked it up since. As far as tennis went, he achieved nothing.

To give him some slack, this kid had no knowledge of universal energy. He didn't understand how his misguided purpose communicated negative energy to the Cloud, and how that negative energy came right back to him.

Allowing: Seeing the doors of opportunity open and taking the steps to go through them.

We are fortunate because we now have the information, and the tools, to help us overcome fear and doubt. We know what to do to get our vibration to rise to a higher level. We also know that life will constantly throw adversity in our paths. And we understand that it has to be that way. Without adversity we wouldn't be able to choose what we want, or don't want, in our lives.

I look at it this way: our higher minded souls decided to come into these human bodies to explore and create the life we imagined, and now we must use the physical mind to enjoy the ride.

We know that, because we're sending positive energy to the field, the field is going to send positive energy back. But are we prepared to receive it? And when we do receive it, what are we going to do with it?

WHAT

Allowing is maintaining our wanted frequencies and keeping them open for manifestation. It's getting into the new flow of our inspired lives. It's cooperating with the universal energy, and letting the bliss we sought stay at the forefront. It's seeing the doors of opportunity open, and taking the steps to go through them.

Atlanta Braves' pitcher, Jesse Biddle, whose picture is on the cover of this book, by the way, ran into some significant adversity a few years ago. One of his challenges was getting back in shape after Tommy John surgery – a surgical procedure in which a healthy tendon extracted from an arm (or sometimes a leg) is used to replace an arm's torn ligament. Another was perfecting his technique. He knew what he was doing wasn't optimum, but wasn't sure how to fix it.

I had the pleasure of coaching him, and I'm proud to call him one of my "kids." Jesse bought in to the RedOps tools, and now any resistance he had that translated into a less than optimal performance, is at a higher level.

To play professional ball, the physical body has to be functioning at 95–100%. If you don't have that, and are only at 90%, a higher mindset can fill in the gap.

This is an example of how *allowing* works. When tough times come, and they will come, we can't get

Without the discipline of inspired vision, we won't have the gumption to allow adversity to roll off.

bogged down in the contrast. That's where our physical minds will chip away at us, saying things like, "You're not good enough," or "You don't want to do this anymore." Without the discipline of inspired vision, we won't have the gumption to allow the adversity to roll off, so that we can keep going.

We're always going to have knee-jerk reactions to unfortunate happenings. It's also human nature to hold grudges. These obstacles are like warning signs. Do you know what you're looking at? How are you interpreting it? How do these things make you feel?

Keep in mind, in some cases getting mad can be therapeutic. It will definitely get the energy moving! The point is, if the feeling isn't good, identify it and stop yourself before you increase negative momentum. Instead, realize the adversity and change your momentum to what you want it to be. You don't have time for the negative stuff anyway, because you're working on your future.

Something else to remember is that if we didn't run on energy, how would our hearts keep beating? How would we survive? This world is sustained by a loving presence that stays in place and is constant. If our source of energy were to be thrown off by just a quarter of a degree, we'd all be dead.

Take the lessons learned from quantum physics, philosophy, and religion, and recognize the energy for what it is – a compassionate field, that wants to love us all the time.

Each of us is a satellite dish, ready to take what the energy field is sending. If we let it, those signals will fall into our dish and fill us with light.

WHY

Life can be jam-packed with devastating things. These can be anything from living with a physical impairment or mental illness, to being the victim of a crime, such as an accident caused by a drunk driver.

> *If we didn't run on energy, how would our hearts keep beating?*

Imagine being the parent of a seven-year-old who battled and succumbed to cancer. What about losing a spouse, or having your home burn to the ground?

On a more global scale, think of 9/11, the shooting in Las Vegas, or the tsunami in Indonesia that was responsible for 300,000 deaths. What if you lost someone close to you because of one of these horrific incidents?

How does one deal with the unimaginable? It's tough, especially when no reasonable explanation exists. By no means am I trying to downplay suffering. We've all lost people we love. We all experience hardship. We all suffer. The question is... how do we get through it and keep going? How do we recover?

Some people don't. Some turn to alcohol or drugs. Their lives spiral downwards, getting deeper and deeper into lower frequencies until it seems they'll never be able to pull out.

Once you're in the pit of lower frequency, your subconscious continues to attract and repel. But it's like you've become adrift on an island, and the only people on that island with you are living in similar feelings and frequencies. Most of us have never been inside a crack den, but we've seen them in movies and on TV. Imagine what living that nightmare would be like.

No matter what happens in your life, the loving, compassionate source of energy only says "yes" and gives us more of what we're broadcasting. We are on a heroic mission, like pioneers on the leading edge. This is what we've been built for.

We were well aware of what this life offered when we decided to come into it, and we knew that in time we'd find our way if we chose to. So give yourself a break! Don't dwell on mistakes of the past, or hold on to shame, guilt, or fear. If you could have done better before, you would have. That was then, this is now.

Your inner guide knows your goodness, and the energy that created you holds no grudges. It would be arrogant of our

It would be arrogant of our physical minds to think anything over and above what our inner guide thinks.

physical minds to think anything over and above what our inner guide thinks.

It's never our place to judge, but to have compassion. Because I'm a believer, I know that God looks upon each one of us with love, and I do my best to emulate that. Practicing Quiet Toughness takes me there. It is the way to help lessen the pain of tragedy and find peace.

Back when I was playing football in college, I didn't know anything about the sciences of the mind, meditation, awakening my spiritual side, or anything else discussed within these pages. But something happened back then, a few years before my cancer scare, that was like a wake-up call.

As with many college students suddenly left to their own devices, I thrived on having fun, and wasn't always responsible. You could also say I was a little big-headed, lacking humility, and believing there was no question I would someday be in the pros. After all, I was on full scholarship at a Division I school, and the starting placekicker my freshman year.

Now, my school had a tiered system – a depth chart – for determining top players. This was acknowledged when the equipment manager handed out colored bibs before practice.

The criterion for the color you received was a mix of everything from athletic prowess, to attitude, to academic performance. A white or blue bib was what you wanted, depending if you were on offense or defense. It meant you were first string. Green was like second string, meaning you had work to do. The red bib indicated you were a quarterback, or hurt, which meant hands off.

The worst color to get was yellow. That yellow bib was a sign that things were not going well, and Coach was not happy with your performance. I'll never forget the day I was handed a yellow bib. What made it even worse was that I was the starter in my position. It was the first real slap in the face I'd ever had. My coach was so incensed, he was ready to kick me off the team!

I had a choice to make. I could call my coach all sorts of names and complain that he didn't know how valuable I was. Or I could stop goofing off, and instead get focused and buckle down.

Had I made the first choice, my life would have turned out quite differently, and everything I subsequently achieved would have never come to pass. I might have never finished college or had a successful, fulfilling career. I imagine I would have never studied the sciences as much as I have, and I would probably not be alive today.

At the time, I knew nothing about the sciences of the mind, and I'd never seen an emotional scale, but I remember the journey my emotions took back then. Shame (#22) came on strong, but that turned to anger (#17), not with my coach, but with myself. I worried a lot (#14), was overwhelmed (#11) for a time, but eventually made it to hopefulness (#6), and again found the passion (#2) I'd lost. I loved kicking footballs! You'd better believe I never got a yellow bib again.

We all have free will, and every day we must make choices. I'm confident that most people will embrace and align themselves with the choices they make. And who knows how their lives will change for the better?

One thing is for sure, if you are not happy and believe there must be more to life than what you've realized so far, give these principles a try.

This makes me think of all the wonderful teachers out there, teaching our children. So many of them feel their hands are tied, mucked up in paperwork and red tape. They often struggle to find the excitement they once had for their profession. I guarantee the curriculum will be changing in years to come, and the new curriculum will include what the sciences of the mind are showing us today. Don't wait for our schools to catch up. Be ahead of the game!

Make a decision tree, a flow chart of sorts, where the branches can lead you to new places. You might find that those branches lead you through the RedOps process, and soon you'll be channeling your energy for your higher purpose.

HOW

Somebody once asked me if I tell the kids I coach to meditate. The answer is no, not initially. If I did, they'd look at me like I'm nuts.

My job as the coach, just like any mentor or teacher, is to get to know the student. The physical side usually comes first. By identifying their strengths and weaknesses, then using kinetic physics, I determine a solid approach to improving both their good and not-so-good skills.

We can do things like lengthen or shorten the arm, or take a longer or lesser stride. I can show them what muscles they aren't using in the right order. Slight changes here and there will increase their ability to use their kinetic chain more efficiently. Everyone's muscles work a certain way to protect and attain results. Understanding this is the key to physical success.

For the mental side, I take a similar approach, by observing behavior and asking questions, not only about someone's goals, but about how they feel. My objective is to provide each student with the right advice to boost confidence. I allow the energy field to download that advice to me, and to tell me when a student is ready to go deeper into RedOps tools. But again, I tread carefully. Many people, especially young men, are often skeptical.

One of the barriers of the modern age is that young people are not used to constructive criticism. For some, the only language that gets through is when I tell them to get their heads out of their asses.

Just like raising a child, as a disciplining parent, you have to figure out what techniques work best. For some kids a five-minute time out is enough. Others could benefit from a full day of grounding and reflection.

Determining the right way to motivate an athlete is similar. A good teacher figures out the best way to reach his student, and a little shot of confidence goes a long way toward getting them moving.

This is an important example for everyone, not just athletes. Think of criticism as a type of contrast. No matter your endeavor – doctor, lawyer, artist, musician   criticism will surface. Take it for what it's worth. If you're running on a higher frequency, you'll be able to handle it. Or, if you're running on a higher frequency, that particular contrast may not even show up.

My more serious pupils will be upfront about what they want and say things like, "I want to play major league ball." If they have the physical potential, I will do my best to get them there. These are the times the mental side becomes more important. I look at it from a place of contrast. What's this kid really here for? What can I give him? And in turn, what will I get from our interaction?

In every relationship there's something to be learned. If a particular student doesn't have the mentality for professional ball, something still brought him to me. I may still have an influence on him.

The thing is, he maintains his own vibration until he is ready to receive more. If he is not open to suggestion, there's no way I can insert my will into his mind. The valve has to be open for that to occur. My job is to maintain the highest frequency for myself, offer my best vibration, and know the individual I'm working with can someday do the same. I always maintain my ability to influence.

One of the kids I trained was 6'6". His problem physically was that he couldn't control his feet. While at the plate, he didn't spread his legs wide enough to get the leverage he needed to be grounded. I coached him into a better stance, but he complained he couldn't hit that way. The next thing I knew, his dad got on his case. The father firmly told the son, "If your coach says to do it, then do it."

> *When we change the way we look at obstacles, we begin empowering ourselves.*

The kid got angry. He got back in the batter's box and took three ferocious swings. I said to myself, "If he did that every time, he'd be a first-round draft pick."

Was this a long-term solution to his issue? Of course not. But it did show that when a player can channel his energy into focused action, it's amazing what he can do!

In this athlete's case, the adversity (or contrast) of a demanding father and an insistent coach were exactly what this kid needed to hear in that moment. Since then, he's worked hard, and now he's comfortable in the new stance. If he keeps at it, he'll be a beast.

We're all a little bit like this kid. We don't like the contrast, but often we subconsciously ask for it. Remember, we only get back from the field what we give to it. Like this boy, when finally he stopped fighting us, and instead embraced the recommendation, his batting improved. For just a moment he was able to use his anger to focus in a productive way, and the resistance he was holding on to was no longer a negative component. This is how *allowing* works.

When we change the way we look at the obstacle and not overreact negatively, when we listen and allow life's lessons to come to us, we begin empowering ourselves.

It might be difficult at first. Remember the emotional scale from Chapter 2? Perhaps the obstacle sends us into despair (#22). We channel our minds until we're out of despair, and emoting anger (#17). The next time it happens, we channel from anger to frustration (#10). After that, we move up from frustration to optimism (#5).

Allowing is not a one-time deal. It's a process that you do on a regular basis, over and over again. Life can throw obstacles at you every day, and every day you "allow" them. The ultimate goal is to accept your perceived "bad" view of the situation. Turn it into a positive.

People will say they are who they are, based upon their genes and their environment. Once we know how to control our frequency, we can change our perception of the environment, and by doing so, amend our life experiences so they will be more palatable.

We are energetic beings in a contrasting world. There will always be adversity. Without it, we can't make choices. And without choices, we can't grow.

The process is this:

(1) We ask.
(2) Know that our dreams have already been created vibrationally.
(3) Clear our energetic pipes of debris and allow the answer to manifest.
(4) Take the inspired action and enjoy the experience.

The goal is to look for appreciation everywhere we can. For example, you're stuck in traffic. But hey, you've got a great car, and the song that just came on the radio is one of your favorites. Rather than moan about the traffic jam, bask in the music and comfort of your vehicle. When we react in this manner, we project a higher frequency, and in return, higher frequencies come back.

> *Once we know how to control our frequency, we can change our perception of the environment and amend our life experiences.*

Have you ever encountered a homeless person, perhaps someone you see on the same corner with his cardboard sign every day? There he is again, in a holey jacket with his socks up to his knees. His hair is disheveled, and he's not shaven. You've heard the stories of scammers – vagrants who'll use the money they get for drugs or alcohol. You don't feel comfortable blindly handing this guy money.

But you watch him, going through a trash can outside the Rite Aid. You see him pull out a Styrofoam coffee cup and drink from it. That's a little unnerving – he just drank someone's cold, leftover coffee. But it proves this guy is thirsty and probably hungry as well. It's the moment you begin to see him not just as a scammer on the corner, but as another human being.

This happened to me. I pulled over and gave the homeless fellow some cash. I asked his name. He shook my hand and thanked me. I left him there, feeling better, and knew my vibration had instantly gone up a notch or two.

We talked before about negative people. Like we talked about in the previous chapter, there will always be those who you think of as "a thorn in your side." It's okay to notice this person's unpleasant qualities, but stop dwelling on them, and don't lash out. Instead, look for their better qualities and focus on those. Over time, you'll find the things that used to bug you, don't nearly as much.

This is never more obvious than when thinking of our culture today when it comes to marriage. The divorce rate in the United States is about 40%. And I am sad to say I fall into that demographic. If I had known then what I know now, I would have been less accusatory and more understanding.

Other people will always let us down. This is an undisputable fact. In most cases they're not being malicious or intentionally trying to hurt us. We're all human, and therefore flawed.

At the same time we must realize that our anger is relevant. No matter what the situation, that anger is there to support us in the moment. What we must remember is that if left to fester, that anger can result in fear and a separation from our higher minds. Our higher minds reflect only love and compassion.

Anyone having relationship troubles can benefit from embracing Quiet Toughness principles. Your higher mind will download to you the information you need to make sound choices about your situation.

Our goal should always be to come up higher, to find the compassionate side of ourselves for everyone, despite our (or their) attitude. That's what God does. If we don't emulate that, our frequency will never be as high as it has the potential to be.

I believe that we came into this world, on a grand mission to experience life, so that God could experience it with us. We are part of the same energy that created the world, and when you think of it that way... damn, that's powerful!

God doesn't want us to sit around doing nothing. We were designed to find joy and laughter, achieve success, make love, eat chocolate, have a glass of wine, and relish our lives. When we hear the ocean and taste peanut butter, so does God, and that's just awesome!

Wrap Up

We've broken down the tools of RedOps into five chapters, but even though we set them apart sequentially, they all interconnect. It doesn't make a difference if you struggle with one and have to go on to the next. You're not stuck. Eventually everything will fall into place. Your higher power is always present, and always telling you, "I got this." Just keep listening.

For all of you working your hardest to make things happen, what can you do to change the way you're visualizing your future? Think about your temperament, and how you're broadcasting your emotions out into the energy field. Remember a vibrational alignment is much more powerful than 10,000 hours of honing physical skills. Your higher consciousness opens the doors before you physically arrive.

We're here on earth to create and enjoy life. By reaching above the adversity and seeing it for what it is, we raise our frequency. So, get out there into the world, let your energy flow, cooperate with the universe, allow the dreams you seek to come to you, and live not just shining in Quiet Toughness, but Quiet Excitement!

QUESTIONS AND ANSWERS

The goal in writing this book is to make known to you every facet of the topics covered, which is why I feel it's relevant to include a question and answer section. Many questions might arise while considering the contents of these pages. I've broken them down into five categories: **Relationships & Family**, **Career**, **Finances**, **Health**, and **General**. My most sincere dream is to see everyone out there—not just athletes—pursue and achieve their dreams. That's what Quiet Toughness is all about.

Relationships & Family

How can I convince my spouse or significant other that Quiet Toughness will help our marriage?

First, let me say that asserting our wishes on someone else will only backfire over time. A better way to approach this would be to practice Quiet Toughness yourself, and by doing so, become a glowing example. Setting an example of someone who has their act together goes a long way in convincing others that what you're doing works.

There is nothing wrong with telling your partner you are practicing Quiet Toughness, but if they don't want to participate, let it be. Concentrate on raising your own vibration, and during meditation, seek guidance from your higher mind on how to approach your partner. Downloads will come to you, and these will help raise your own awareness and communicate more effectively.

If my partner doesn't buy in to Quiet Toughness, can I still help him/her by utilizing the principles myself?

As stated in the first question, the energetic laws of the universe tell us that one cannot cause long lasting change in another person by imposing our will onto them. Even though there may be some positive short-term results, inevitably you'll lose a little bit of yourself in the process, and so will your partner.

What you're doing is judging, and judging is dangerous. It's like trying to change matter with matter, an exhausting process with no real result. Each individual must decide to become the person they choose to become.

Consider your own connection with your higher mind or God-consciousness. This is paramount and will trump everything. Our purpose in life is to create with our higher mind so that our physical body can enjoy what we've created.

Significant other relationships are often the most difficult contrast in our lives. This is because your partner—the person you're in the closest proximity with—vibrates at their own frequency, and that frequency won't be exactly the same as yours.

Think of it this way: Imagine two vibrational circles—one of them is you, the other is your partner. How much of the circles intersect? If only 5%, the relationship isn't in harmony. The higher the percentage, the more likely the relationship will flourish. Those with 90% to 95% vibrational similarities are the folks whose relationships endure.

How can I teach my children about Quiet Toughness when they're not willing to read this book?

As most parents will tell you, adult-child relationships can be difficult. Your little humans are growing up, developing physically and mentally, but they're not yet fully mature, and neither are their emotions. Teens especially can be rebellious while trying to figure out this thing called life. Sadly, our school systems don't have any curriculum on the sciences of the mind, so it's left up to parents to become the teachers.

One way to approach the topic is this: Everyone has experienced static electricity at some point in their lives, even our kids. Because they've felt the current, or the shock, use it as example of the energy that makes up our universe. This may make sense to them. But if they're still reluctant to listen, the most important advice I can give is: don't try to ram Quiet Toughness down their throats. Instead use it to demonstrate the greatness within you.

Remember, a teacher always knows their students. Be smart! First, become the person you choose to become. Unconsciously your children will sense your vibration. After all, they come from the same energy source that beats your heart. That means subconsciously, just like you, they already have a built-in knowledge of their higher mind.

All of us are looking for answers, whether we realize it or not. If you discuss Quiet Toughness with your children, but get no response, a simple act like leaving this book on the coffee table, maybe with a bookmark or a folded down page, can go a long way. A time may come when out of curiosity your child picks up the book and starts reading. You never know!

As stated in Chapter 2, one of the primary lessons in RedOps is accountability. How do we teach our children to be accountable for their actions?

We teach them by example. Accountability begins with self-discipline, which parents need to practice and hone every day. Remember, when our children are in their formative years, they're learning by observation, and parents are the central influence.

Our children's next greatest influences come from their peers and school environment. In many ways, school is great, but when it comes to the sciences of the mind, to use a euphemism, this is where we threw the baby out with the bath water.

For me, it's not a religious issue; it's a science issue. When prayer was banned from schools, it took away the opportunity for our kids to have scheduled time to pray, meditate, give thanks, and even daydream about a life that feels good to live.

No one wants to have religion forced on them or to be told how to pray, and that's not what I'm advocating. What's missing is structured "quiet time." This is imperative for helping our children tap into their subconscious and find their mindfulness. Without that reinforcement in their education, for parents, teaching these concepts can sometimes feel like an uphill climb. Our goal should be to provide our children with the information, explaining to them how universal energy works, and be patient and observant.

Notice our children's inner guides taking shape as they grow. Accountability will be there, but in some cases it may need more parental prodding than others. But we also must be careful. We don't want our children's accountability or motivation to be fear-based. A disciplined approach will inspire them to achieve dreams first in thought, and then by following through with inspired action.

Because our children's emotional development is still in process, how do we get them to understand the emotional scale?

This all flows from our children gaining an understanding of energy and information, self-discipline, and accountability. One way to help children recognize their emotions, and ultimately reach their higher minds, is to encourage positive behaviors and feelings. This also raises self-esteem. A child who understands who they are and feels good about themselves has confidence. As previously conveyed within these pages, confidence goes a long way.

In our culture today, parents consider it a duty to correct children's "bad" behaviors. The goal being that our children will learn from the punishment and not repeat the behavior. People will say there is a time and place for discipline, and tough love is important. Remember that these so-called "bad" behaviors are the result of our kids making decisions with their physical minds, rather than their higher minds.

For parents, watch how we say things and how we react. The emotion we put behind our words and actions is the best lesson for our kids. Instead of thinking of our response as a punishment, try softening the approach with a loving, compassionate mindset. And remember "discipline" can always be turned into a positive learning experience.

What lesson does the child take away from the situation? How should they approach a similar situation in the future? How do they feel about it? The last thing we want is for our children to be completely disconnected from their higher minds or emotions. This leads to sociopathy—children who grow up to have no regard for themselves or others, an unfortunate and difficult path.

How can Quiet Toughness help to deal with a friend or family member who often gets defensive?

You've heard the old saying, "First time, shame on you; second time, shame on me?" That may be a bit harsh, but talking to someone who is defensive provides a good example of *contrast*. Rather than looking at the situation negatively, consider what you can take away from it, keeping in mind that adversity helps us grow.

What if you're trying to help someone out by sharing something from Quiet Toughness principles? Don't go into it with the mindset, "I know something you don't." Remember, no one likes to be told what to do—even you. Get to a higher vibration and be tactful, be creative.

You cannot assert your thoughts and opinions onto another person's experience and think everything will come out peachy keen. Instead, let the defensive person see the changes Quiet Toughness has made in you. The next thing you know, they'll be asking, "What pills are you poppin'?"

All kidding aside, we can use our higher minds to guide us during conversation, recognizing opportunities to perceptively share our wisdom.

How can Quiet Toughness help with overbearing personalities?

An overbearing personality is another example of *contrast*. Keep in mind, there is a reason for the experience. Think of it as a test you have to pass in order to move on to bigger and better things. Another way to look at this is to ask yourself, "Is something in the vibration I'm giving off reflecting back to me?"

Figuring out the "why" of difficult situations is not always easy. Remember the universe is based on attraction, and that means your vibrational energy is being matched. Once this understanding is achieved, the change in your vibration could send an overbearing person vibrating right out of your life.

How can Quiet Toughness help when we know someone doesn't like us?

If someone doesn't like you, it's their issue, not yours! You have one job, and it's not being a people pleaser. Your job is to get yourself into vibrational alignment with your higher mind. Only then can you live in the bliss you've created. Only then will you return to conscious awareness of your physical body. Only then will there be a shift in vibration that will improve your mood or temperament. Your physical mind will walk hand in hand with your higher mind, and the higher mind doesn't play down to anyone whose vibration is energetically low.

Career

How do we deal with difficult co-workers in the work environment?

You understand *contrast*, and that there is a reason for it, right? Maybe you have a knee-jerk reaction to a fellow worker. It's time to let that contrast teach you something, to ponder how your responses are reflecting back on you, and finally to come up to a higher vibrational level. Then you can chuckle about the situation and go on with your duties. Eventually, that troublesome co-worker will be transferred, or you'll realize you're in the wrong job and move on to something bigger and better. The answer is to get your physical mind in alignment with your higher mind. Once there, you'll form a vibration that you'll find refreshing.

How do we deal with a difficult boss in the work environment?

I like to look at others this way: There are no "bad" people; there are only people who vibrate at a low frequency. When you educate yourself about universal energy and the sciences of the mind, you understand what's happening, which enables you to deal with almost anything effectively.

Perhaps you take a moment to review the emotional scale in Chapter 2, and use it to figure out where you're oscillating. Then you do what's necessary to move up the chart. It's okay if you don't immediately jump into the top five. Take baby steps. Reach for an emotional vibration you can realistically attain. If you find yourself raging (#19), maybe jump up to anger (#17). Just make sure you deal with your anger in a manner that doesn't hurt anyone. Go into the woods and scream. Or sign up for boxing lessons. That punching bag sure can take plenty of hits! As the anger is released, your vibration will rise. Maybe you still can't get into the top five, but hopefulness (#6) is a pretty good place to hang out.

As a boss or manager, how can Quiet Toughness help motivate employees?

Everything in the universe is energy and information. This formula is the same for all of us. What that means is that everyone who works for you has the same feelings you've had. Do your best to be conscious of this. This is similar to how teachers must get to know their students. Are you building a business team? What inspires the people on your team? Determining this will certainly make a difference.

Keep in mind, different people are inspired by different things. Remember the circles we discussed earlier? Not everyone intersects with your circle the way you'd like them to. Some employees are "team players" and others couldn't care less about you or the business. Their only interest is the paycheck. You can always ask yourself why you hired that person in the first place. Or, why you are in a job that has a person like that working there. Sometimes we make mistakes, and those mistakes become the contrast we learn from. In the future, you'll make the right decisions *before* a "wrong" decision can manifest into something difficult to handle.

As a school teacher, mentor, or coach, what are some ways Quiet Toughness can help me better communicate a students' difficulties to easily offended or overprotective parents?

Be kind! Keep yourself in the highest vibration possible. Remember what other people think is not really your business. Of course no one likes criticism; praise feels far more rewarding.

The problem is we've been taught to think negatively, so as a physical being, running into these situations is inevitable. Don't devalue yourself or your teaching methods because of one person's opinion. Take the "hit" of criticism for what it's worth.

If you haven't been practicing Quiet Toughness, it may feel like your day, week, or even your month has been ruined.

Buck up, little camper, and remember whatever doesn't kill us makes us stronger. Take inventory of your thoughts, feelings, and emotions, and make adjustments as needed. Most of all, *never* devalue yourself because you may not have gotten something right. Your higher mind loves you and wants the best for you. Remember that when you enter into your next Quiet Toughness session.

Public speaking is considered one of the greatest human fears. Can I utilize Quiet Toughness to overcome fear of public speaking?

Fear ranks the lowest on the emotional scale, coming in at #22. Fear/powerlessness is the absence of love. If you're one of the lucky people in the world who enjoys public speaking, you may still feel butterflies in your stomach before you stand up. Those butterflies are normal.

Whether you *want* to be in front of a room full of people or not, we all care about our presentations. If you're experiencing a tremendous amount of anxiety, it's usually one of two things: (1) you're not prepared and unsure of the information you're getting ready to present; or (2) your confidence/self-esteem is low. Lack of confidence can even cause panic. It comes from being disconnected from your power source (higher mind). At that point, physical matter (the audience) becomes a bigger deal than your compassionate, confident higher mind.

Scientists would call this "the wave." For some, a pat on the behind might be the boost you need to get on your feet. Others may benefit from verbal reassurance. If it's available, take it. I'd also like to propose that being afraid is akin to arrogance, in that your low frequencies are trying to fight against how your higher mind, or God-consciousness, sees you. I suggest you return to Quiet Toughness, experience the unconditional love and compassion offered by your higher mind, and *never* think badly about yourself!

If we need our current job to pay the bills, knowing that our dream job isn't lucrative, how can we justify pursuing it?

In this situation you may just have to grit your teeth and do what you have to do, but remember you're not alone. I think we all struggle, or have struggled, with this one. You may recall I shared the story of the tumor in my stomach, the medical difficulties that arose because of it, and that I almost lost my life. At the time, I had a job I couldn't see any way out of, and it wasn't what I wanted to be doing. This was also before I had a full understanding of Quiet Toughness. Since honing my Quiet Toughness, I've made the changes necessary to move myself in a more desirable direction.

My advice for this one is similar to something I said earlier about children. I said to not necessarily criticize when you catch them doing something wrong, but find the lesson in it. Encourage them more when they do something right. My point is you've created momentum that has led to desperation. This is the time to practice Quiet Toughness as often—and as soon—as you can. That will change your vibration, give you the information you need to move forward, and build up momentum going in the opposite direction the road you want to be on.

A word of caution: You cannot change your current physical world with the same mind that created it. To even attempt this would be impossible. One needs to go from working harder (motivation) to inspired action, where you are not merely responding to external stimuli, but you become a new person, taking your cues from your higher mind. You're doing what your higher mind tells you to do based upon how good it feels.

Through Quiet Toughness, you've quieted your mind in order to practice mindfulness techniques. You've pulled away from current sensory perceptions, leaving behind what you see with your eyes, feel with your body, hear with your ears, taste with your tongue, and smell with your nose. Now, you're allowing your imagination to hand you the pieces, until you have a full picture of how you would truly like to live. The organizing properties of the higher mind have kicked in and have begun to reorganize the proteins in your brain, as well as the physical components of the world. Remember, all matter is created from the quantum field. It manifests back to us the vibrational energy that we placed into it.

Finances

It's been said that money is the root of all evil. How do we differentiate between seeking financial gain for the betterment of others and not being self-seeking?

Respectfully, I must disagree; money is *not* the root of all evil. Don't let anyone guilt you into this trap. Money can be a great thing. The key is knowing how to properly handle it. Money mismanagement can become stressful. This is a lesson I've learned from personal experience! Please remember that every one of us is selfishly oriented. We want things in our life, right? Think of it this way: In our world, nothing good happens when money is not circulating. Money should be thought of like energy, just like everything else, hence the reason we call it "currency." Money contains information as well. Abraham Lincoln will buy some things while Benjamin Franklin can buy more things.

Quiet Toughness works really well here, as we are continuously broadcasting signals about money. Those signals are either that we have money, or we don't. The danger is this can be a double-edged sword. Because we are attraction magnets, what we broadcast into the quantum field is what manifests in our lives. In other words, whatever we send out vibrationally, we get back in our physical reality.

Don't we all do things because, in the end, they make us feel better? If we are not living the life we've imagined, Quiet Toughness will be the game changer. Mindfulness training gives us the chance to retreat from our current life, so that we can emotionally imagine, and thereby feel, the life we want.

Consistent repetition is paramount. The organizing intelligence of the universe wants to get involved in your life. Let it! Depending on how much momentum you have going the "wrong" direction, that will determine how long it takes to turn things around. As soon as you begin to emotionally feel better, you've received the sign that you're on your way.

You want to always stay connected to the "good feeling" or the "higher vibration." Then look for the information coming to you that will enable you to navigate prosperity. Remain in the feeling of appreciation and excitement as often as possible, no matter what is going on around you. An attitude of appreciation and excitement sends out those vibrational signals, and people and events will already be moving into position to bring your desires to fruition. I guess this is where the saying, "attitude reflects your altitude" comes from.

In today's society, money is important to survive. How do we pursue our own dreams if our dreams take money that we should be spending on family and/or friends?

There was a time in our history where stealing was prevalent, whether it be cash or cattle. These days we have identity theft and cyber terrorists. Many complain about our government taking money for taxes. And daily we hear stories in the news of break-ins and burglaries. I think we often fall into a trap of thinking we're stealing from our family or friends if we spend money on ourselves, and we feel guilty. I propose that as long as you're pursuing dreams that come from your higher mind (not your physical mind), you shouldn't feel guilt. Those dreams, once manifested, will enable you to do more for family and friends than you've ever done before.

Stick to Quiet Toughness rules. Stay in the vibrational frequency of abundance, and you will come to understand the power you possess. If we practice high vibrational states as often as possible, and incorporate the information downloaded to us, we will always fly higher than the altitude of loss.

Can Quiet Toughness help us earn more money?

Of course it can. Please refer back to the answer to the previous question as well. But I caution you to watch the word "earn." It has a lower frequency associated with it. This is not necessarily from the word itself, but rather the feeling the word represents. We live in an abundant universe that hears our request the moment we ask. From there, the universe begins to set up ways for us to receive back what we've asked for. But we have to be in the right vibrational frequency to realize it. The understanding of how money works and its relationship to our own energy is undeniable.

If a thought has been downloaded to you that will require you to spend money, and by doing so you'll be going into debt, do you go ahead with it?

The "feeling" behind the issue is what I recommend you get in touch with. Generally, of course, it's not a good idea to go into debt. That being said, there are many things that consume our dollars—like mortgages or car payments—that are necessities, yet these put us into debt. Being in debt can be highly stressful. Think of people who have to negotiate deals on their credit cards just to pay them off. Yikes!

But that doesn't always mean going into debt is "wrong." Again, it depends on the feeling you get when you spend, or rather the feeling you got *before* you spent (hopefully you meditated on the decision before following through).

As with anything else in life, if we are not practicing the art of wholeness or completeness, then we're not making decisions with our higher mind; we're making them with our physical mind. In this life, the truth is there really is no material thing that we *must* have. What we're actually doing is telling ourselves these things are "must haves" and then acquiring them under the guise that they'll make us feel better. This is our physical mind at work. There is nothing wrong with having things. But, if we buy simply to satisfy a low vibrational need, rather than a high vibrational want, then we are falling into muddy water.

I will be the first one to admit that I have mismanaged money in the past. These days before I make a purchase, I wait for a "hell yeah" moment. If I don't get one, I don't buy. My short and sweet advice: Get a "hell yeah!" from your higher mind first.

Health

Can Quiet Toughness help to overcome bad habits, like smoking or drinking?

Absolutely! To give a better answer, I want to take this a step farther. In Chapter 3 of this book, I talked about the heart condition I had—the result of radiation treatments for cancer thirty years before. The emergency procedure doctors did to unclog my arteries was successful initially, but then the stenosis (clogs) started to form again. I was informed that my only real hope was a new heart. This is when I began my Quiet Toughness training.

Through meditation, I was able to change the makeup of proteins in my brain. My mind entered into the quantum field, which is the energy field surrounding my body, also referred to as "the higher mind." Think of it in terms of wave energy. Instead of using the physical particles, I became no one, in no space, and in no time. This allowed the cells in my body to be in coherence once again with my God-consciousness, so that they could reorganize and return to the fully functioning cells they'd been, the way they were meant to be.

This change follows the science of neuroplasticity. Like the physical laws of the universe, there are physical laws that govern the human body. Together the two can become a powerful team, depending upon where you are in your vibrational frequency.

So to answer the question, yes, Quiet Toughness will assist you with alleviating smoking or drinking habits, but only if you're in the right frequency when approaching the issue. Any issue that deals with physical health has to do with not only our biology, but our perceptions of our biology and environment. What that means is if you are functioning at a low energetic frequency, it is unlikely anything will work, including substance abuse treatment facility intervention or smoking cessation aids, like nicotine gum or the patch.

PLEASE NOTE (AND I SAY THIS AS LOUDLY AS I CAN): Quiet Toughness is **not** a replacement for Western Medicine. Yes, you can help yourself overcome difficulties and even illness, but please, please, please **don't ignore your doctors**. Although we are learning to use meditation to help cure diseases, we're still in the infancy stages, just beginning to understand how the mind can facilitate healing. Quiet Toughness is a tool that can be used in conjunction with medicine to augment positive treatment results.

How can Quiet Toughness help with dieting and exercise?

This and the previous question remind me of a friend of mine. A few years back, she quit smoking, and as with many who quit smoking, she ended up gaining weight. This didn't sit well with her, so she started smoking again. As those extra pounds fell away, she joked that she was on a "diet by cigarette." A few years later, even though she still smoked, she gained the weight again. So much for that diet by cigarette, right? Perhaps she would benefit from a little Quiet Toughness training.

Although she may make jokes, I think we all agree health is important. In the United States, obesity is so common it's considered an epidemic. I don't know of many people who don't struggle with weight and diet issues. Even if you have the metabolism of a beanpole, you still want decent muscle mass. We know how the body works physically, right? If we eat properly and exercise, we should achieve results. But what if you're someone who, no matter what you do or how diligent you are, that scale doesn't move? Something is clogging you up, just like me and my arteries. Those clogs are like poison.

The key to any of this is you can't just pay attention to your physical body; you have to pay attention to your vibration. When the two work together, change will occur! Think of energy and information. Having the proper mindset is the beginning of wisdom, and the beginning of seeing the results you want to see. If your goals are big, such as you want to participate in Iron Man competitions, then the energy field will give you the knowledge and the contacts you need to get you into the best shape of your life. All you have to do is listen, and then follow through with inspired actions. Know how you want to live your life, use the laws of the universe to attain it, and while you're on your way, enjoy the ride!

When facing serious illness, if our doctor doesn't agree with Quiet Toughness principles, can we still follow them?

Please refer back the "PLEASE NOTE" on page 85. Certainly you can continue to follow Quiet Toughness, knowing that everything here is based upon science. It is unfortunate that your doctor doesn't buy in. But I also am certain running into this scenario would be rare. I've never heard of a physician who didn't recommend keeping a positive mindset when dealing with a serious condition. I also believe most doctors do recommend meditation or prayer to help alleviate stress.

We are only in these physical bodies of ours for X number of years, some longer than others. This is not about cheating death. At some level we all realize a serious illness, if not treated, could end our physical existence. Just remember, when you understand the scientific principles of energy, you realize energy cannot be destroyed, only transformed.

What should we do if our doctor's recommendations go against the Quiet Toughness principles we practice?

Run! I'm just kidding. Doctors are trained in the hard sciences of disease and healing, and we wouldn't want it any other way. In my case, before Quiet Toughness, my energy was so far off track that if it weren't for my physicians, I wouldn't be here. Western medicine saved my life. Doctors are incredible people, and deserve respect. However, getting back to the question, again I propose that this scenario would be rare, if not non-existent. But let's look at this from a different perspective. Remember the laws of momentum? If you're practicing Quiet Toughness, you're fixing things in your physical body *before* they get broken. That would mean those invasive procedures and medicines might never be needed.

Mental illness has become more prevalent in our society today. What impact can Quiet Toughness have on those suffering illnesses such as depression, bi-polar disorder, schizophrenia, sociopathy, or psychopathy?

I spent more than 30 years in the behavioral health field, studying psychology, as well as observing and working with clients. Do I believe Quiet Toughness can help those suffering from mental illness? Yes. Thousands of testimonies have been given by people who have been able to circumvent such difficulties through mindfulness training, meditation, and prayer. But, we must also remember that when dealing with mental health issues, we're dealing with biological and neurological disorders.

I believe that under the right conditions, neurological hardware can be rewired. In others cases, results may only be attained through a combination of medication and mindfulness training. And in severe instances of sociopathy or psychopathy—where the patient does not feel emotion— Quiet Toughness may have no direct impact since the individual has no desire to practice mindfulness training.

At this time in our history, we are behind in understanding how all this works. Even so, science is now showing us the path, and we are making strides. The bottom line here is that no matter what the diagnoses, Quiet Toughness will cause no harm. It can only improve outlooks and give rise to contented, more fulfilled lives.

Substance abuse of both illegal and prescription drugs runs rampant in society today. Will practicing Quiet Toughness enable people who suffer from addiction to overcome it?

Addiction is another area in which I worked extensively during my career. I have seen many disgusting things as a result, some too gruesome to share. I also saw families torn apart, and it saddened me every time. Do I know Quiet Toughness can help? Again, the answer is yes. But it will be a longer road than it would be for the average person.

When it comes to addiction, we're talking about people so mired down in lower frequencies, it can seem impossible to break out, especially if the addiction has controlled them for years. But I also don't want anyone to be discouraged, because it can be done! The trick is recognizing the issue and truly wanting to overcome it.

If an addicted person goes into fixing their problem half-heartedly, success is unlikely. In that circumstance, they're attempting to change their physical reality, but only using their physical mind to do so. In order to change physical reality, you must use more than the physical mind. Through the higher mind you can experience what a healthy body feels like. Once you appreciate having a healthy body, then the proteins and neuro receptors in the brain begin to change.

I'd also like to add a note for family and friends of people suffering from addiction. Being in a relationship, whether familial or not, with an addicted person can be debilitating. Quiet Toughness will help. I'm not suggesting we can stop the addiction, because the only person who can do that is the addicted person. I'm also not saying Quiet Toughness will end the trials we deal with as a result of the addiction. What Quiet Toughness will do is help us to remain of sound mind, steadfast in our determination, and positive about the future.

By raising our frequency, we're empowering ourselves, not only in maintaining a higher emotive temperament, but in receiving downloads of information that will better enable us to deal with our addicted loved one, as well as steer us toward the right resources for help. Quiet Toughness allows us to be still for a moment and quiet our minds, so that we can stop seeing the disease, but rather see the goodness and truth that still exists in others. In this manner, we will have come a long way in our humanity!

General

How do we remain humble and still boost self-confidence?

In actuality, humility and self-confidence are one in the same. When we understand the rules that govern our universe, we find ourselves living in a mindset of completeness. We have nothing to prove, and because of that we only have good feelings to give away.

Think of it like this: How could you want to hurt someone when you, yourself, feel whole? You're residing in frequencies of appreciation, freedom, and love. There would be no reason to put on airs or brag. Bullying or seeking revenge wouldn't even enter your thought processes. All of those feelings come from fear. In the absence of fear, we're naturally both humble and self-confident. Hence the name of this book—Quiet (humble) Toughness (self-confidence).

Will Quiet Toughness help to overcome low self-esteem?

There's only one answer here—absolutely! As you practice Quiet Toughness, you ascend to the higher frequencies and confidence rises right alongside. People with low self-esteem worry that if they talk about their accomplishments, they'll come across as egotistical. This is similar to the last question about humility. There is a difference in tooting your horn to make yourself feel better, and tooting it for the benefit of others. While residing in higher frequencies, your tooting won't be showing off. When you're coming from feelings of appreciation and empowerment, everything you do or say becomes beneficial for others.

What is the difference between meditation and prayer?

Semantics. That's the short answer, anyway. If you're someone who doesn't believe in God, *per se*, yet you agree with everything we've discussed about universal energy, then you might be uncomfortable referring to meditation as prayer, and that's okay. Perhaps another way to differentiate between the two is that unless you're in "deep" prayer (picture Tibetan Monks), people praying don't necessarily enter fully into a meditative state. Think of a church setting, where the minister is at the front, praying. The folks in the pews may have their eyes closed and their heads bowed, and they're listening, but they're not meditating. That doesn't mean, however, that people don't spend time with God in a quiet place in their homes, "deeply" in prayer. In such instances, in my opinion, prayer and meditation are one and the same. You could also consider it this way: Meditation is focusing on the circumstance in life you want to see come to fruition. The feeling that goes along with it is the prayer.

For people strong of faith (no matter what religion), how do we juxtapose our religious beliefs with Quiet Toughness principles?

I don't think there needs to be a differentiation between the two. "God," "Our Creator," "Life Force," "Energy Field"— whatever name you want to use for the higher power that surrounds and controls every living on earth and everything in the universe—is entirely up to you. I prefer "God-consciousness" because this term is a reminder that the force is loving and compassionate—something I think we all tend to forget at times.

I would like to share that, like many others, I've received not-so-great advice from people who are supposedly "strong of faith." We see and hear things in the news that are done in the name of "God" that don't reflect a loving compassionate being at all. This can cause us to scoff at, or become alienated from, religion. Whether you go to church or not is your call. What you believe religiously is your call. Here in the United States, we're fortunate to have freedom of religion, and that means we can practice whatever we want to practice. Quiet Toughness is not about religion or a specific belief system. Rather, I like to think of it as a way to enhance whatever belief system we choose.

Most religions consider the God they worship to be compassionate and loving. Aren't these the same frequencies we achieve through Quiet Toughness? We should never feel guilty or squeamish about using the word "God." I remember as a young boy at Catholic school hearing, "With all thy getting, get wisdom!" By practicing Quiet Toughness, by raising your frequencies, I think wisdom is coming on pretty strongly.

Between family and job obligations, our time is limited. How do we justify making time for Quiet Toughness?

Leverage, leverage, leverage! Consider this: How many hours do we spend stewing over grudges, stressing over finances, complaining about unfair situations at our job? I propose that instead of spending hours upon hours climbing out of holes like these, we take the time to do mindfulness training. Who knows? Perhaps we wouldn't have fallen down those holes in the first place?

Let me leave you with this: If you're working your fingers to the bone, how long do you think it will be before doctors are working on those fingers? I'm confident that once you get into Quiet Toughness and begin to realize its benefits, you'll have no problem making the time for it.

Will Quiet Toughness make us more emotionally aware or wiser?

How can you not be more aware or wiser when you're in sync with the force that creates life? As Albert Einstein said, "I want to know the thoughts of God; the rest are details."

Do you have a question not answered here? I welcome all inquiries, or even if you just want to say hello, I'd love to hear from you. Please connect with me through:

CJ DiRoma
Station Avenue Productions
cjdiroma@stationave.com
(215) 644-8171
230 Kings Highway East, No. 167
Haddonfield, NJ 08033

Appendix A

GLOSSARY OF TERMS

Aura – the energy field that is specific to and immediately surrounds a human being or animal, often described in size, color, and/or shape.

Cell Biology – (*also* **cytology**) the study of the structure and function of cells, the basic units of life, and includes chemical composition, life cycle, metabolic processes, physiological properties, and interactions with the environment.

Electromagnetic field – a combination of an electric field and a magnetic field, extending indefinitely throughout the universe, and one of four fundamental forces of nature. It is produced by electrically charged objects, and affects the behavior of all objects in its vicinity.

Energetic Field – used to describe the energy that surrounds all living things. It also extends to and encompasses the universe, and is often referred to as "universal energy field (UEF)."

Energy – the invisible quantitative property transferred to an object to cause it to move or react. There are many types of energy, including **kinetic**, **gravitational**, **electric**, **magnetic**, **elastic**, **chemical**, **radiant**, **thermal**,

available, and **renewable**. All living organisms require energy to survive.

Epigenetics – the study of transmissible or inherited characteristics not associated with DNA, by noting variations that affect gene activity in the progeny of cells and organisms.

Frequency – the number of occurrences of a repeating event per unit of time, used to determine rates of oscillatory and vibrational phenomena, including sound and light waves.

God-Consciousness – an understanding or belief in connection and adherence to a supreme being who created and controls the universe and all its elements. Synonymous with "Higher Mind."

Higher Mind – the part of human consciousness that conveys and receives emotional energy from the energetic field. Combines and conceives thoughts, ideas, and beliefs between the subconscious and physical mind.

Inner Being – the complete consciousness of a person that includes the subconscious and physical mind, as well as the physical and spiritual body. Synonymous with "soul."

Meditation – the practice of focusing on a particular object, thought, or activity to achieve a mentally clear and emotionally calm state, as well as to empower self-realization and enlightenment. Often used to reduce stress, anxiety, depression, and pain, and promote psychological, neurological, and cardiovascular health.

Neuroplasticity – (*also* **neuroelasticity** *or* brain plasticity) the ability of brain cells to alter, move, transfer, strengthen, or weaken. Causes include environment, age, activity, thought processes, and emotion. Changes in plasticity impact development, learning, memory, injury, and health.

Physical Mind – reacts to and creates conscious thought processes that are perceived solely from influences within the physical realm.

Quantum Electrodynamics – (QED) the study of how light and matter interact, mathematically describing the exchange of electrons and photons.

Quantum Physics – (*also* **quantum mechanics** "QM" *or* quantum theory) the study of the behavior of matter and energy at molecular, atomic, nuclear, subatomic and smaller microscopic levels, and the probability of movement within the universe.

Soul – a person's subconscious moral or emotional identity, believed to exist before birth and live on after physical death.

Spirituality – generally used in Christian doctrines, referring to mental and physical connection to the Holy Spirit. It is also used non-religiously to denote connection with the inner-self, and the quest for moral and ethical growth, as well as a connection with invisible dimensions.

Vibration – the oscillation of disturbed matter, whether fluid, solid, or an electromagnetic wave. Also refers to a person's emotional state or the atmosphere of place.

Zen – from Buddhism, a person's instinct, intuition, insight, self-control, and meditative practice as it relates to their spirituality.

APPENDIX B

HELPFUL LINKS AND RESOURCES

Below are website links for several renowned doctors and scientists. I encourage you to seek out videos on their sites and listen to what they have to say. Topics cover everything from quantum physics and cell biology to the healing properties and advantages of meditation.

Dr. Joe Dispenza – https://drjoedispenza.com

Bruce Lipton, Ph.D. – https://www.brucelipton.com

Wayne Dyer, Ph.D. – https://www.drwaynedyer.com

Gregg Braden – https://www.greggbraden.com

Dr. Deepak Chopra – https://chopra.com, or https://www.deepakchopra.com

Sarah Lazar, Ph.D. – neuroscientist, discusses how meditation can reshape our brains: https://www.youtube.com/watch?v=m8rRzTtP7Tc

The science of heart math – https://www.heartmath.com

ABOUT THE AUTHOR

CHUCK BUSHBECK is a former professional athlete, baseball scout, sports television and radio talk show host, author, and cancer survivor. After a 30-year career in behavioral health, he opened the Full Armor Training Facility and began formulating his RedOps program. Today, when he is not at either ESPN's studio or coaching, he can be found traveling the country providing inspirational talks to rising young athletes and the general public.

Would you like to know more of Chuck's story? Find out about his rise to athletic excellence, and how he refused to quit while battling cancer in the heartwarming, inspirational novel, ***Full Armor***, available at certain retail locations and on Amazon.

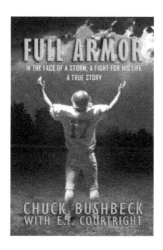

CONNECTING

Do you have any questions or comments for Chuck? He would love to hear from you.

To connect with Chuck, please contact:
CJ DiRoma
Station Avenue Productions
cjdiroma@stationave.com
https://www.stationave.com
(215) 644-8171
230 Kings Highway East, No. 167
Haddonfield, NJ 08033

An Excerpt from

FULL ARMOR

Chapter 1 – Rising Warrior

"When he was about two, to keep him from running outside, we put a leash around his waist and tied it to the sofa leg. The next thing we knew, he dragged the sofa across the room. I told my wife, 'That was kind of a bad idea there'." —Chalie Bushbeck

Labor Day, 1974

Somebody stunk, the cloying odor of sweat. The kid with the white blond hair in the middle of the pack got a potent whiff when his nose jammed into an armpit, but he didn't care. For him, the growls and shouts of "Get him! Take him down!" were like lighter fluid.

He barreled on, the soles of his sneakers digging into hard-packed earth, pushing, shoving, to get past five bodies, most bigger than him. He made it through two postage-stamp front lawns and into old Mrs. Smith's yard. Somebody's head cracked on his jaw. It smarted enough to make him grunt. An elbow rammed into his ribs. His thighs burned, but no way was he giving up.

The rending tear of fabric came from his T-shirt. A sweat-drenched arm slid against his equally sweaty back, skin on skin. Whoever it was let go, giving him the opening he needed. He plowed ahead, while one by one the rest of the boys dropped.

The blond barreled down the hill to the sidewalk, momentum spilling him against a parked car. Baking in the sun, its fender seared like a lit stove. Spinning away, he grinned and raised both arms in triumph, holding up the football he'd carried.

The neighborhood boys played many games—stickball, hockey, a plethora of nameless others, and of course, baseball. Between them, they only had one baseball, and it was held together with black electric tape. Their bat wasn't in much better condition. When it broke, they'd nailed it, and then wrapped it in electric tape, too. Their football was half-deflated with most of the laces missing.

"You suck, Chuck!" one of them bellowed. The kid leaned over with his hands on his knees and panted. Two others plopped down in a rare patch of grass. Franny, the last to give up, reached up to the limb of a dogwood tree and dangled.

"Wanna go again?" Chuck asked, running fingers through his hair. It was as sweat-damp as the rest of him.

They did go again. After that, Chuck gave up his place as ball carrier to Franny. Taller than Chuck by a couple inches and strong, the opponents nailed him. But at that point they were in the alleyway. Franny's elbow was scraped raw, and Chuck ended up with a bloody shiner. The left eye, this time. Everybody had bruises and cuts. They always did, and they wore those battle scars proudly.

The heady scent of charcoal grills lingered in the air, a tribute to the holiday weekend. A radio blaring through an open window updated them on the game. The Phillies were at Pittsburgh in the middle of a double header. The first game had been a dud—the Pirates triumphed, 11-1. Now, at the top of the second inning of the second game, the Phillies were up, 3-1.

Except for Chuck and Franny, the rest of the guys had to go home before their mothers started yelling. By the time Chuck realized he still had the football, the kid it belonged to was at the end of the alleyway. Chuck hollered after him and punted.

The ball sailed high over the kid's head, across the intersection, and plunked on the roof of a house.

"Sorry!" Chuck called out.

The kid flipped him the bird.

"I'm thirsty," Franny said. "Wanna get a soda?"

"Sure." Chuck shrugged, an attempt to fix his torn, stretched out T-shirt.

The two ambled on, past row houses, duplexes, and apartments, toward Dayton's corner store three blocks down. The sidewalk was cracked and choppy, caused in part by tree roots growing underneath. A radio coming through another open window updated them on the game, now in the bottom of the second with no runs given up.

"Don't you have a soccer game after school tomorrow?" Franny asked.

"Yeah," Chuck said. "You gonna stay?"

Franny wasn't on the soccer team. He'd tried out, but didn't make it. "Don't know," Franny hedged. "It's the first day of school, ya know."

They were both 14, going into their freshman year of high school. Most of the kids from the neighborhood went to public school, but if you were a Catholic boy living in the Mayfair section of Northeast Philadelphia, you enrolled at Father Judge.

They turned at the next corner and saw the front lawn picnic going on across the street. Parents stood around a smoking grill, while younger kids romped through close knit yards, a dog loping along. But these things didn't hold Chuck or Franny's attention. Sitting on a porch stoop were four teenaged girls. Two would soon be Bambies—Catholic girls who attended St. Hubert's, the sister school to Father Judge.

Franny cocked his head that direction and in a low voice, asked, "Is that Maribeth?"

She was hard to miss with her long dark hair and feminine curves, but she wasn't looking their way. None of the girls were.

They were too busy jabbering. From all the way across the street, Chuck and Franny heard their laughter ring.

"Yeah, that's her," Chuck told Franny. "Let's go say 'hi'."

"And crash the party?" Franny sounded dubious.

"Why not?" Chuck grinned. "I can invite her to my game."

"Show off," Franny scoffed, and he picked up the pace. "Come on. Mr. Dayton's daughter might be working. She's smokin'."

Chuck cast one final glance at the porch, then had to double step to catch up to his friend. Just before they reached the next intersection, they overheard another radio blaring. In the top of the third inning, the Phillies were still winning. With a stoked kick to their step, they waited for the traffic to clear and carried on.

On the corner in front of the store, was a gathering of MaBrowns. A half dozen guys from the gang, garbed in jeans and T-shirts, kept watch over their turf. But to Chuck and Franny, MaBrowns weren't a threat. They were just older guys from the neighborhood.

"Yo, Chuck and Franny!" one of them hailed.

Another tapped by his eye and mocked, "Cut yourself, did ya, Chuckie? Nice shirt."

Chuck looked down. Flapping across his collarbone was what used to be part of a sleeve. His exposed shoulder was already pink with sunburn.

"Rough and tumble, eh?" the MaBrown guy asked.

"Yeah," Franny and Chuck replied at the same time.

Bells jangled as they pushed through the door into the corner store. The familiar odor of moldy wood overwhelmed, but the blasting A/C felt good. They were out of luck as far as getting an eyeful of the proprietor's daughter though. The only person behind the counter was old man Dayton. Perched on his stool and hunched over a magazine, he didn't look up.

They grabbed soda bottles out of the refrigerator in back and were on their way to the counter when Franny dug into his pocket.

"Crap," he whispered. "I only have a couple pennies. I swear I had more."

Chuck had enough change for his bottle, but not two.

"Run," Franny said.

"What?"

"Run!"

"Heck no. My dad—" The loud jangle of bells cut Chuck off. Franny was already through the door.

Chuck dropped a dime and six pennies on the counter and rushed after his friend, calling over his shoulder, "Sorry, Mr. Dayton."

"I'm gonna tell your father about this, Chuck Bushbeck!" Mr. Dayton hollered.

Chuck flew by the MaBrown guys and caught up to Franny halfway down the next block. They took one look at each other and busted out laughing.

Franny guzzled from his bottle and said, "I gotta get home for dinner. My mom's gonna kill me anyway. Look what else was in my pocket. I forgot to take it."

He held up a triangular yellow pill for Chuck to see, then tossed it to the gutter. "Don't tell her I did that."

Chuck took a swig of soda and the two strolled on, passing the cookout again. The younger kids still romped and the adults were there, but the stoop where the girls had been was vacant.

"Figures," Chuck mumbled.

Moments later they were in the alleyway again. Chuck's house was third from the end. Franny's was farther down.

"See ya, Franny," Chuck called as he slipped through the backdoor.

As always, his mother was in the kitchen, an apron over her flowered top and summer slacks, spatula in hand. Her name was Dolores, but everyone called her Dolly. That day her shoulder-length pale locks were clipped at her nape. By the age of 12, Chuck had outgrown her, and now towered by several inches. This didn't stop the narrow-eyed glare—the one that told him she was mad enough to start swinging. His behind knew the sting of her spatula well.

"Really, Chuck?" she said. "How many shirts have you ruined this summer?"

At least four, he thought. To his mother he said, "Not sure."

"Let me see your eye." She was already in front of him, grabbing his chin to angle his head down and inspect. "Why don't you go take a shower and clean up? When you come back, I'll put Neosporin on that. Are you hungry?"

"Always." Chuck grinned. "I take it Dad won't be here for dinner tonight?"

"No. He's on nights tonight and tomorrow. Your sister's joining us. Now go." The spatula circled and jabbed toward the stairs.

Chuck rumbled on. Dolly liked blue, so everything in the house was blue—the carpet, the sofa, the recliner, the drapes. He took the steps to the second floor two at a time.

Soon he was downstairs again, across the table from his hippie sister. Kathy was blonde like him, except her hair was long. As usual she had it parted in the middle, held down by a thin band around her forehead. Tonight her pants were zigzagged striped bellbottoms.

She was seven years older and no longer lived at home. Sometimes Chuck missed her. Kathy had a lot of friends, both guys and girls, and Chuck had liked hanging out with them. The other thing he missed was sneaking into her bedroom to steal her albums. She was always yelling at him to give them back.

While his sister and mother droned on about girl things, Chuck filled his trap with meatloaf and potatoes. A serving of lima beans wasn't going anywhere near his fork. One night, a few years back, he'd been stuck in his chair until midnight, the pile of nasty green things on his plate untouched. It was one of the few contests his parents let him win.

"You ready for school tomorrow?" Kathy asked.

Chuck looked up. "Yeah."

Kathy smirked. "It's a big day for you... first day of high school. Are you nervous?"

"Nah."

"He has a soccer game in the afternoon," Dolly chimed in. "He made the varsity team this year."

"And he's just a little bitty freshman," Kathy teased.

"Yeah? So?" Chuck retorted. "Coach thinks I'm good enough."

"Stop, you two," Dolly scolded. "Kathy, are you coming to Chuck's game?"

"Can't. I have to work. Sorry."

Chuck was glad when the dishes were done and he could get away. His mother and Kathy turned on the TV, but he grabbed the latest *Baseball Digest* from the coffee table and headed upstairs. In his bedroom, he cranked up the radio and plopped down on his bed. The ambiance there was much better. Across the room were the shelves his dad had put up so Chuck would have a place to display his trophies. He had a lot of trophies.

The rest of his walls were covered with Eagles pennants and Broad Street Bullies posters, including a couple with action shots of his favorite Flyers—Bobby Clarke, Bernie Parent, and Dave Schultz. Chuck had plenty of Phillies mementos too, and stuck in with the trophies was a baseball autographed by Johnny Callison, caught at Chuck's very first game, when the Phillies still played at Connie Mack Stadium. That day they beat the Mets, 3-1.

On the radio he listened to the end of the current game. Despite the Phillies' initial lead, the Pirates came back and won it, 7-4.

"Boneheads," Chuck whined, then he leaned over and turned the dial to a music station. Aerosmith's *Dream On* belted out of the speakers and Chuck sang along, changing the lyrics to fit his disappointment. "Yeah, keep dreamin' Phillies..."

Early the next day, he rose to deliver newspapers. He had two paper routes, the *Philadelphia Inquirer* in the morning and the *Bulletin* in the afternoon. After his *Inquirer* run, his father still wasn't home. Chuck changed into his school uniform, including coat and tie, wolfed down the pancakes his mother made, checked to make sure his cleats, shin guards, and socks were in his duffle bag, then rushed out the door.

"Don't forget your lunch!" Dolly called after him, spatula waving.

Father Judge was about a mile from their house. Chuck didn't get far before he was joined by Franny and a few other boys. They marched on another block until a car pulled to the curb. Joey Cugine, one of Chuck's soccer teammates, was in the passenger seat. Mrs. Cugine leaned over and asked through the opened window, "Do you guys want a lift?"

The sedan was already full, but the boys piled in anyway. A little bumbled rearranging and five of them fit into the backseat. Two others crammed up front with Joey and his mother.

She dropped them off in front of the school's Vietnam War Memorial. Behind it was the flag pole, and beyond that the enormous three-story, tan brick building. The boys ambled up the steps to join the other 2000+ students roaming the halls.

Chuck went through the motions, but all he really cared about was the soccer game. As soon as his last class ended, he hurried to the locker room to change.

Before heading out to the field, Coach McDonald made the team congregate in the chapel. The coach prayed and gave a pep talk. The Father Judge Crusaders were taking on the dominant team in the league, Cardinal Dougherty. Dougherty had won three consecutive championships, taking the Catholic League titles in '71, '72, and '73.

Pumped-up Judge players spilled out of the chapel and headed to the field. On the way Chuck spotted his mother, along with other parents, striding up the hill beyond the track, the place where most spectators gathered. In the past the only games—soccer or baseball—she'd missed were if she had to work. She was a part-time switchboard operator for Bell Telephone. Chuck knew his dad wouldn't be there— he'd be home sleeping since he was working the night shift.

Kickoff soon came, and Dougherty was as tough as their reputation. Chuck wasn't a starter, so he watched from the sideline, cheering on his teammates and hoping Coach would sub him in. At halftime the Crusaders were down 3-0, and Chuck was still waiting.

The second half was as grueling as the first. Even though the Crusaders had closed the gap by one, they were still down two goals. Nearing the final minutes, Coach McDonald yelled, "Chuck, you're up. Next sub."

Finally he had his chance.

Chuck ran out and took his position in the backfield. He'd been playing soccer since age 6, and he was pretty good. He wouldn't have made the varsity team otherwise. But going up against Dougherty's bigger, more skillful juniors and seniors— some ranked top in the state—was like nothing Chuck had ever experienced. Within the first minute on the field, a Dougherty forward plowed right over Chuck, and kept advancing toward the net.

Chuck scrambled, chasing after his opponent, and another defender joined him. Double-teaming the Dougherty forward was the only way Chuck could sneak in and steal the ball. He dribbled, looking for a Judge midfielder or forward, and when he saw a teammate open, delivered a solid pass.

Once they had possession, the Crusaders' offense desperately tried to narrow the margin. Spectators on the hill began to chant, "Judge! Judge! Judge!"

A Judge forward got behind a Dougherty defender and ripped a shot toward the corner of the net, but the Dougherty goalkeeper dove and deflected it.

Seconds later, the end-of-game whistle blew. Dougherty won.

As the dejected Judge players came off the field, Coach McDonald said, "Don't let this loss get you down. You guys played a good game and held on against a tough team. Be proud of yourselves today."

Chuck knew all that. He just wished he'd had more playing time.

He and his teammates were on their way to the locker room when Joey Cugine bumped Chuck's shoulder and gestured with his head.

Casually strolling along the track were three girls dressed in matching brown jumpers and saddle shoes—the St. Hubert's uniform. Chuck stopped, his gaze settling on the one in the middle, the one with long dark hair—Maribeth.

"Hi, Chuck," she said.

"Hi," he said back.

The Bambies continued on, and Joey plucked Chuck's arm. "Chuckie's got a girlfriend." Several teammates snickered.

The girls didn't look back, but they giggled and kept going through the gate and across the parking lot, disappearing around the side of the building. Chuck had to hurry to catch up to his teammates.

Moments later he and several of the guys came out of the locker room, freshly showered and again wearing their school uniforms. Together they traipsed through the grass to the front of the building where they could hear whistles and shouts from the fields across the street.

Directly across was the baseball field, and beyond that, the football field. Football players were still at practice, some now on the baseball infield working with blocking sleds. The rest were running drills.

But Chuck didn't really look at them. His mother was standing on the sidewalk. Beside her, parked at the curb, was a brown Plymouth Fury police cruiser.

"Oh, you gotta go. Later, Chuck," Joey said. He and the rest of the guys took off.

"See ya," Chuck called after them, and he started toward the street.

It didn't occur to him until he was almost there that he might be in trouble. He'd completely forgotten about the soda he and Franny stole, and he wondered, as his steps slowed, if old man Dayton had called his dad after all.

Chuck's father, Charles Bushbeck, was leaning against his squad car in full police regalia, complete with rimmed cap, badge, and belt wreathed with handcuffs and sidearm.

Dolly was the first to notice Chuck coming. "There he is," she hailed in a proud mom voice.

"Hi, Mom. Hey, Dad," Chuck said, and he asked his father, "How long have you been here?"

"Long enough to see you out there." His dad pushed off the car and took a step closer. "Nice shiner under that eye. That's not from the game today, is it?"

"Nah. From the alleyway yesterd—" Chuck barely got the words out.

In a move too swift for him to dodge, his father's arm swung, grabbing Chuck in a headlock. The knuckles of Charles Bushbeck's free hand ground into Chuck's scalp.

"Quit it, Dad," Chuck railed, struggling to get free, but the effort did little good. His father was too strong.

"For goodness sake, Chalie," Dolly scolded. "You'll mess up his uniform."

"Yeah, yeah," His dad got in one last noogie and let go. "You did well out there today. Nice slide tackle. Couple good passes. Dougherty's the best team in the league, ya know. Those guys are top notch. But what about school? How'd that go?"

"Good," Chuck said absently.

"That's it? That's all you're gonna give me?" Chalie's eyes narrowed. "I need more details."

Chuck shrugged. "Just thinking about the game. Wish Coach would've put me in more."

"You could always try football." Chalie gestured across the street. Linemen were facing off in their stances. The next moment the air was filled with grunts, growls, and the crack of colliding shoulder pads.

"Nah," Chuck said. "I like soccer."

"What if you do both?" Dolly piped in. "You could be a kicker like... oh... what's his name... Tom something or other."

Chuck knew who she meant. Watching the Eagles play on TV was a standard Sunday afternoon event in their house during football season. Tom Dempsey was their placekicker and held the record for longest field goal in the NFL. He'd kicked the 63-yarder in 1970 while playing for the New Orleans Saints.

"I wouldn't be allowed to do both, Mom," Chuck explained. "The teams practice at the same time. And I wouldn't want to be a kicker anyway. Kickers are wimps. If I play football, I'd wanna be on defense. I'd wanna *hit*."

Chalie chuckled. "All right, tough guy. I'm not on until seven. How 'bout we go *hit* some ice cream?"

"Ice cream before dinner?" Dolly balked. "Really?"

"It's a special occasion." Chalie winked at his wife. "Today Chuck proved he could hold his own with the best of 'em."

ACKNOWLEDGMENTS

I would like to send out my appreciation to the following talented and remarkable people: Jon Shevelew, Elizabeth Courtright, MaryBeth Heilmann, Demi Stevens, Jesse Biddle, David Biddle, Jim Sims, Doug Shimell, Jake Ferry, Brian Courtright, Chuck Bechtel, and CJ DiRoma. Without you, this book wouldn't exist. I am blessed to have you in my life. I am humbled to consider you part of my team. Thank you from the bottom of my heart.